SEC
PSYCHOLOGICAL STRENGTH

Ten Driving Lessons for a Healthy Mind and Happy Life

Steve Daily, MS

Kansas City

Published by
CreateSpace

ISBN-13: 978-1979905930
ISBN-10: 1979905932

CONTENTS

Introduction

Hi. I'm glad you've decided to read, Secrets of Psychological Strength*. I've made the choice to talk to you at times in a direct manner. I want to be more personal than most writers. When I'm talking to you directly, I will be using this font. If this annoys you, then feel free to skip those parts in this font.*

I have no idea as to how many readers I might reach. It may be just a handful, or if I'm really fortunate it may end of being many. What matters is not the number of people who read it. You and each reader are truly what counts.

I really want you to make positive changes that will bring you more happiness and peace of mind. As a therapist I know that my clients can change in two basic ways. They can change what they do, and by changing their behavior their thoughts and feelings often follow. They can change their thoughts and beliefs, and in doing so their behavior and feelings tend to follow. I believe these same principles apply to you as a reader.

I hope you will read all or at least enough of my book to benefit from my experience working as a psychologist for over thirty-five years. I will do my best to help you to build your psychological strength. If by reading this you end up making even a couple of positive changes in your life that help you grow, then my writing it will be worthwhile.

This book is NOT written for persons who have it all together and command excellent willpower in the pursuit of achieving meaningful goals. It is written for the everyday man or woman who has dreams, but continually falls short of realizing those dreams. It is intended for those who feel stuck in life, and frequently have no idea where their time has gone. It is written for persons caught up in worry and other traps of thought. This book is for those needing to build their psychological strength so they can find life less stressful and more satisfying.

Psychological strength is the ability focus, to think and act wisely, to be aware of one's emotions and not be completely overpowered by them. It is the ability to bounce back from disappointments and setbacks, and to use stress in a positive way to achieve worthwhile goals. Psychological strength also involves the interpersonal skills of being able to talk in an honest and direct manner, to actively listen and understand how others think and feel, and the willingness to show vulnerability when it is safe to do so.

I believe that reading this book and applying skills you learn can help you to become both physically and emotionally healthier. It can help you move from a state of victimhood to one of empowerment. You will discover skills to better manage your thoughts so they will work for you instead of working against you. You will be more able to walk a middle path and free yourself from rigid thinking and overreacting.

This book can teach you a strategy to conquer procrastination and form better habits to be more productive and experience feelings of accomplishment. You will acquire skills for shielding yourself from the negative comments of others. You will discover effective communication skills to assist you in making requests and setting boundaries. You will also see that trying to do too much for others can rob them of learning and cause you to feel resentment.

As you read the last several chapters of *Secrets of Psychological Strength*, you will understand that mindfulness practice can help you to dwell less on past regrets and reduce worry about the future. You will have more peace of mind as you learn to respond mindfully to difficult situations instead of reacting impulsively. You will feel more confident and have improved self-worth as you develop habits of gratitude practice and as you use personal affirmations to guide your life.

You are invited to read this book with some healthy skepticism. Please try out the ideas, strategies and skills offered in this book to determine which ones are helpful to you and which are not. An effort has made to give practical suggestions for implementing ideas presented in each chapter. It is in doing things differently that a person often masters a new idea, and uses that idea to improve his or her life in some way

The ten chapters in this book summarize a number of key ideas that the author has used to help his clients better understand life and to make positive behavioral changes. Much effort has been made to put forth the ideas in an easy to understand and succinct manner. I wish I was a more talented writer, but I have come to accept that completing something to benefit others is better than contemplating a great work that never gets off the drawing board.

I hope you have found some areas mentioned in my introduction that you would like to learn more about to improve your life. Most people want to be physically healthier, and there are ideas for doing this

in chapter one. Almost everyone I know struggles with procrastination. I offer some interesting ideas in chapter five for overcoming this obstacle to productivity and personal growth. I invite you to take a look at chapter one, and then decide if it is worth your while to read further.

Chapter 1: Mental Strength

Keeping Enough Gas in Your Tank

SECRET: Practicing physical and emotional self-care is essential for having a healthy mind and happy life.

I am starting my book on the topic of physical and emotional self-care, because it is so important. I've learned that there are times when getting good exercise can help persons manage depression better than taking anti-depressant medications. Please pause and think about how well you take care of your body. Do you exercise routinely? Do have good eating habits, and eat healthy foods? Do you practice good sleep hygiene?

I want you to understand that you can directly improve your psychological strength by improving your physical health. I also want you to learn that there are specific things you do that deplete your energy level, and other things that build it back up. Finally, I would like you to develop a routine for improving your emotional self-care, and I will encourage you to make more time to have fun.

There is one more thing I wish to share. As I read I can get lost in thought, and may miss important ideas. Because I want you to get what I consider important, I am going to speak to you in this font and check in with you to see if you are getting the important stuff.

In the pursuit of becoming psychologically stronger, mental strength is the first of ten important concepts to be explored. Mental strength is just one component of psychological strength. After reading chapter one you will have a better understanding of the importance of mental strength in living a happy and productive life. You will discover the benefit of maintaining a healthy emotional balance. By learning what factors deplete mental strength, you will be in a better position to guard against wearing down too quickly. The value of routine physical exercise will be explained. Benefits of restorative sleep will be discussed. Before ending the chapter, you will learn how emotional self-care and healthy eating also increase your mental strength.

Defining Mental Strength

Mental strength is defined as the level of emotional stability and clarity of thought that a person exhibits at a given time. When a teacher is enthusiastic and uses clarity of thought to communicate ideas to her students in an exciting and intelligent manner, she is exhibiting a high level of mental strength. A low level of mental strength may be exhibited by the same teacher if she is exhausted at day's end, feels angry over her daughter getting up after being put to bed, and automatically yells at her and swats her behind. Improving one's mental strength is essential for good psychological health.

Have you ever noticed that some individuals seem to have a high level of energy, exhibit good emotional control, and accomplish day-to-day goals giving them a sense of fulfillment and happiness? Have you observed others who more often than not feel drained, are quick to lose their temper, feel a lack of accomplishment, and experience more misery than joy? Persons falling in the first category would be described as having good mental strength and emotional balance, while those falling in the second lack mental strength and emotional balance.

Healthy Emotional Balance

It is important for us to maintain an optimal level of ***emotional balance.*** Too much emotionality often results in persons acting in a way that tends to be dangerous. It's like going to a gas station and leaving the pump going and finding the automatic shut off failed. There are several gallons of gas underneath your car, and all it takes is a spark and you can imagine the rest. Too little emotionality causes persons to feel drained and to lack the motivation to be productive. It is like running out of gas, because you forgot to fill up your tank.

One person may be highly anxious before taking an important test. As a result of having excessive anxiety the night before the test, that person may pace the floor and worry about failing the test. If that anxiety remains high during the test, he may experience mental blocking and be unable to answer questions he normally knows. A second person that is depressed may put off studying, because she feels too fatigued and doesn't care if she passes the exam. If she makes it to the test at all, she is likely to give up quickly and not perform well. Both of these persons would have a low level of mental strength due to poor emotional balance.

Factors Depleting Mental Strength

Let's explore some key factors that deplete mental strength. Low glucose levels in the blood lower one's willpower and mental strength. If your body is not adequately fueled, you will have difficulty thinking clearly and regulating your emotions. Fatigue and lack of sleep also contribute to decreased mental strength. Way too often persons do not get an adequate amount of sleep, or fail to experience the restful and restorative sleep needed for optimal mental strength. Illness, headaches, and physical pain deplete mental strength as well. Lack of exercise is often a significant factor that leads to a decreased level of energy.

In addition to physical factors, there are a number of psychological factors that drain an individual's mental strength. Worry and rumination (negative repetitive thinking) are at the top of the list. Some anxiety that leads to problem solving or proper planning is useful. Worrying over and over about things that are outside your control intensify your level of physical arousal and can gradually exhaust you. Developing skills to identify and counter your negative worry thoughts may prove quite useful in developing improved mental strength, and will be addressed in a later chapter.

If you are beginning to think that this talk about mental strength and emotional balance is boring and has nothing to do with you wanting to be happier, then I want you to get the following idea. If you treat your body right, it will be there to support you rather than defeat you when you most need it.

A second point is that when our mental strength is depleted, it is not the time to make important decisions or have that crucial talk. If you are in conflict and your emotions are rising, it is the time to use the STOP skill. If you have problems managing intense emotions, using the STOP skill can change your life.

The STOP Skill

The study of neuroscience shows that the amygdala in the brain triggers a fight-flight-freeze reaction when we perceive danger. Our bodies are hardwired to go into survival mode when the brain detects a life-threatening situation. In this mode our heart rate increases, digestive systems shut down to provide more energy, adrenalin is released to make us stronger, and the stress hormone cortisol is pumped into our body to keep us on high alert.

In the cave man era this response would help save your life if you needed to run swiftly to escape an advancing wild animal, or if you needed to fight an enemy to survive. In the present day we often go into survival mode in situations where our life isn't threatened, but our ego is. We may become intensely emotional when arguing with a child or parent. We may even become unglued in a debate about politics or religion. In those situations, the use of the STOP skill could be most helpful.

The STOP skill is an acronym for four steps to be taken when you are beginning to lose it. When we go into the survival mode, there is a disconnect with the prefrontal cortex in the brain that helps us make wise and compassionate decisions. Failure to use the STOP skill may leave you without the needed tool of intelligent and empathetic thought. Here is the STOP skill.

STOP

Stop before you make things worse. (Avoid going into the fight-flight-freeze reaction when your life isn't threatened by telling yourself to ***stop!***)

Take several deep breaths to calm your body and quiet your mind. (Deep breaths help you to relax your body and quiet your mind. You may need to take other actions if your emotions are too intense like rubbing cold water on your face and the back of your neck).

Open your mind to better options in responding. (When you have calmed down, consider what would be healthy or wise options for responding in the current situation).

Proceed with respect and compassion. (Act in a wise way that will allow you to be respectful and to show compassion to others and yourself).

Good Self-Care Is Essential

An essential key to improving one's mental strength and emotional balance is ***self-care.*** Self-care is defined as the intentional act of caring for one's physical and emotional health. In caring for one's body, self-care may involve eating good foods, getting adequate sleep, exercising, taking slow deep breaths, avoiding excessive alcohol or harmful drugs, and receiving appropriate medical care. In caring for one's mental or emotional health self-care may involve identifying and avoiding ineffective worry and rumination. The following are ways to increase mental strength: talking with persons who are affirming and supportive, reading books that are uplifting, laughing, and having fun. It is important to treat oneself as a friend, and not as an enemy. When persons engage in self-care, they typically experience happiness, more energy, and they have increased peace of mind.

Importance of Exercise

One of the most important things we can do to improve our mental strength is to engage in routine exercise. You do not need to run marathons, pump weights, or pay large fees on gym memberships to get the health benefits from exercise. Walking is inexpensive and an easy way to get physical activity. Exercise has been shown to decrease both depression and anxiety. It also has an array of other benefits to the human body that include lowering blood pressure, strengthening the heart, improving brain health, and extending life expectancy.

I have played racquetball three times a week for years, and routinely walk outdoors in good weather and use a treadmill during the cold of winter. Most people are more likely to follow through with an exercise program if it is one they enjoy. It also is helpful to exercise with a friend or loved one. Some people are more likely to walk, if they walk their dog rather than walk alone. ***The best type of exercise is one you enjoy enough to continue.***

If you have health concerns, it would be wise to consult your physician before embarking on a more rigorous exercise program. Most adults would benefit from having about 150 minutes of exercise a week. If you are walking to decrease depression, it is helpful to walk at a brisk rate for thirty minutes at least three times a week. In *The Depression Cure,* Stephen Ilardi outlines therapeutic lifestyle changes that have proven effective in helping persons overcome depression. He emphasizes that exercise is medicine for the brain and body. He also writes about the benefits of exposure to sunlight, eating healthy foods, socializing, lessening rumination, and improving one's sleep hygiene.

Exercise isn't a four-letter word. Please understand it is important for both your physical and psychological health. What are ways you might enjoy getting some exercise? Where would be an enjoyable and safe place for you to walk? Do you like to swim, bike, play tennis, or work out at a gym or in the comfort of your home? When you watch TV, could you do stretches or walk in place during commercials. Set a realistic goal to get some exercise. Doing this one thing can improve your health and the quality of your life.

Benefits of Restorative Sleep

Lack of restful and restorative sleep leads quickly to depleting our mental strength. It interferes with both our ability to think clearly, and it robs us of the energy needed to act in a productive way. Most people require approximately eight hours of sleep to refresh their brain and replenish their body to perform at an optimal level.

How much sleep do you routinely get? How often do you experience symptoms of sleep deprivation, such as, dozing off during talks or lectures, feeling tired or exhausted, or experiencing a lack of energy and motivation to do things you want to do? If you answer yes to any of the above, consider taking steps to improve your sleep hygiene.

Common things that interfere with sleep include watching disturbing TV programs in bed or shortly before retiring to bed. The news often focuses on negative events that had happened that day. Worrying about life stresses has kept many people awake at night. Drinking alcohol may make it easier to fall asleep, but the person awakens as alcohol leaves the bloodstream and may have difficulty returning to sleep. Being in physical pain is the number one reason for awakening at night, and not being able to fall back to sleep. Wise use of pain medication may help with this problem. Lack of darkness and noises also make it difficult for persons to sleep.

Seven Tips for Improving Sleep

1. **Make your bed a desirable place to sleep.** In your mind visualize your bed as welcoming and comfortable. Imagine how good it will feel when you go to bed and lay between the sheets. Fully appreciate the comfort of being in your own bed.

2. **Strive to go to bed and get up near the same time each day.** Allow your body to become conditioned to a sleep routine.

3. **Journal an hour our or two before going to bed.** You may write about things you have been worrying about, and a brief plan to use to address those concerns tomorrow or at some future time. Write a "coping ahead plan" where you journal about handling a difficult situation you need to face with skill and courage.

4. **Prepare for bedtime by doing something that is relaxing to you physically and that will help quiet your mind.** Instead of watching the news with murders and tragedies, read a funny book.

5. **If you do not fall asleep after 15 to 20 minutes, get out of bed and do something until you feel sleepy.** Consider watching a comedy on TV, doing housework that won't disturb others that are sleeping, or playing a video game like Free Cell or Mine Sweeper.

6. **Try keeping your eyes open until you fall asleep.** I realize that sounds strange, but we often start thinking too much when we shut our eyes. For some people attempting to keep their eyes open actually helps them fall asleep.

7. **Remember a positive experience in detail.** An example might be remembering a day on vacation where you went to the beach. Try to remember getting out of bed, showering, dressing, eating breakfast, driving to the beach, parking, etc.

Healthy Eating Improves Mental Strength

Nutrition is another important factor in building our mental strength. Eating healthy foods fuels our bodies to be able to do the work we need to do. As mentioned earlier, lowered glucose levels deplete our willpower. Have you ever noticed that you tend to become grumpy and think less clearly when you have gone too long without eating? Your brain is part of your body, and it requires nourishment to function properly. Most people would benefit from eating more vegetables, fresh fruits, and less sugars.

How might you improve your eating habits? Have you ever practiced eating only three times a day at mealtimes? Have you ever stopped drinking pop, eliminated bread from what you eat, or added fresh fruit to your daily food intake? I have read many books on healthy eating, and I will share the one that I have found to be most helpful to me. It is titled, Bright Line Eating: The Science of Living Happy, Thin and Free, by Susan Peirce Thompson, Ph.D. If you struggle with eating, I would suggest reading it.

Emotional Self-Care

It is important to understand that we do not have an unlimited supply of emotional energy. If we deplete our emotional energy, we will experience decreased mental strength. If we spend too much time worrying about a friend's health, we are making an unwise expenditure of our energy. If our dad criticizes us and we keep going over his hurtful words in our mind, it will quickly deplete our energy. If we continue to engage in wasting our emotional energy on things outside our control, we will soon feel drained and our mental strength and emotional balance will suffer.

Emotional self-care often starts with becoming aware of the many things we do that deplete our emotional energy. Identifying negative worry thoughts and refuting them is important, and will be discussed in some detail in the chapter on belief management. Spending less time listening to negativity is another step. This may involve listening to less judgmental TV shows, reading less negative articles, and spending less time with persons who are highly judgmental and critical of others.

Use the next page or take a blank piece of paper and at the top write: OUT OF MY CONTROL. Now draw a relatively small box in the center of the page and write: IN MY CONTROL. Next write down all the things you spend your time worrying about or brooding over in the portion that is outside your control. Those are the things that drain your mental strength, and you need to work on lessening the time you spend there. Now turn to the smaller box containing things within your control. It will contain your thoughts and actions in responding to the world around you. That is where you need to focus your time and attention to be psychologically strong.

OUT OF MY CONTROL

IN MY CONTROL

An important element of emotional self-care is making time to have fun. Persons who are happy have more mental strength and are more productive. Make a conscious effort to balance work and play. You will actually achieve less in the long run, if you focus only on work.

Do some simple things throughout the day you enjoy. Make time to laugh and have fun. Be able to see humor in some of the crazy things you do. Be forgiving of your mistakes, and at the same time take steps to be more mindful of what brings you and others a sense of joy. You may enjoy going for a walk, reading a book, talking with a friend, sipping a cup of hot chocolate, or engaging in a sporting activity.

Thank you for reading my chapter on physical and emotional self-care. I hope there was something beneficial you learned that you will put into practice. Now is the time for you to focus on doing at least one of the following five suggested activities. Select the area that would benefit you the most and start doing it. I hope you discover that small steps lead to big and lasting changes. After you master doing one activity consistently, add another activity.

Activities to Build Psychological Strength

1. ***Get adequate exercise.*** Step up your exercise program if you are getting less than 150 minutes of exercise a week. Please consult with your personal physician if you have health concerns. Exercise is medicine for our body and brain.

2. **Improve your sleep habits**. Make a list of several things you might do to improve your sleep hygiene. Visualize feeling happy and comfortable in your bed. Develop a bedtime routine that helps to quiet your mind.

3. **Eat healthy and remember the benefits of keeping your body properly fueled.** Eat a healthy breakfast to start your day off right. Eat nutritious foods with enough protein to keep your glucose level in the optimal range.

4. **Focus spending your energy on things within your control.** Don't waste it on rumination and negative thinking. When you have intense negative feelings, be aware of the troubling thoughts behind the feelings. Ask yourself, "Are these thoughts factual, or are they just stories I'm making up in my mind?"

5. **Make time to do fun things alone and with others.** If possible kill two birds with one stone by doing an activity that is fun and provides exercise. Many do this by biking, swimming, playing competitive sports, or hiking on a beautiful trail. Develop hobbies you enjoy, such as, drawing, reading, photography, crafts, or movie watching. Do things with family and friends that are enjoyable.

Chapter 2: Belief Ownership

You Behind the Wheel

SECRET: Taking ownership of one's life and beliefs leads to feelings of empowerment and effective living, while blaming leads to feelings of victimhood and misery.

I want you to feel empowered and enjoy the benefits of being a responsible person. You may have already mastered this secret, but if you haven't it can be a life changer. Do you at times feel like you're a victim? Do you make up excuses when you fail to keep a commitment? Do you pout and feel sorry for yourself? If you answered yes to any of the above questions, then it is important to study this chapter. If you already do a good job of belief ownership, then reading chapter two may help you to better understand those who are trapped in a mental state of victimhood.

Accepting full responsibility for one's thoughts, feelings and actions is an important step in developing psychological strength and in having a healthy mind and happy life. When persons believe they are victims, they feel helpless and powerless. Persons who believe they are responsible for how they respond to life's challenges are more likely to take steps to solve their problems and feel a sense of accomplishment.

The Story of Ted

When Ted was a child his father was an alcoholic and punished him unfairly. Today at work Ted and his coworker had an important project due. Ted had completed more than his share of the project and had done quality work, but his work partner had not. Ted's boss yelled at him, and reprimanded him for not completing the project. On the way home from work, Ted was pulled over by a motorcycle policeman and ticketed for having a left turn signal light that was burned out. He had no idea before being pulled over that the light was out. While grilling pork steaks on the deck, the propane ran out leaving the steaks only half cooked. After this happened Ted was thinking life sucks, and it's not fair when his wife dropped a glass pitcher of lemonade on the kitchen floor. He went in and yelled, *"Can't you do anything right?"*

Guess what? Thinking life sucks and isn't fair, won't change Ted's childhood, put him in good graces with his boss, repair the turn signal, or finish cooking the pork steaks. In fact, that thought intensified his negative energy to a dangerous level and resulted in him yelling at his wife. In that moment, Ted's ***emotional balance*** was out of whack, and his ***mental strength*** was low. Now the key thing to understand is that if Ted takes responsibility for his belief he will be in shape to make things better, but if he blames others he will make things worse.

How do you think his wife would respond if he says, *"I'm sorry I yelled at you, <u>but</u> I wouldn't have to yell if you'd be more careful. Besides you know I grew up with an alcoholic dad who always yelled at me. You know I can't help it. Besides my boss yelled at me for not finishing the project. I worked really hard, but that jerk Jerry didn't do his part."* You can get the idea without me going on and on.

Now how do you think his wife might respond if he says, *"I'm sorry I yelled at you. That was totally unfair. <u>I worked myself up into a state of frustration and anger by thinking negatively about several things that happened to me today.</u> Let me help you clean up. Then I need to go get a bottle of propane to finish the pork steaks and pick up a light bulb for my car. Sorry we're going to be eating a little later than planned."* If you guessed the second would go over better with his wife than placing blame on everything that went wrong, you're absolutely right.

You Behind the Wheel

When you are driving down the road, you better focus on driving responsibly. It would make no sense to plow into the car in front of you, and say it was the other person's fault because he was driving too slow. If your light just turned green, it would not be advantageous to run into a car that was trying to squeeze through the intersection. A good driver is going to be focused and do his or her best to avoid accidents.

In life, many people have mistakenly learned that they feel better by blaming others for all of their problems. The immediate consequence of blaming may slightly reduce guilt feelings, but the long-term consequences lead one to feel victimized and angry. ***In most cases the person who does not accept responsibility for one's behavior, is less happy and more stressed than the one who does.***

What Is Belief Ownership

Belief Ownership is assuming responsibility for what you choose to believe and for the resulting feelings and actions that follow. In most situations, we can think in a way that will cause us to feel in one of three ways.

1. When Ted was ticketed for driving after dark without a working turn signal light, he could have thought in a way that would have caused negative feelings. *"You, stupid cop! All you're doing is collecting revenue for the city."*

2. He could have thought in a way causing him to have positive feelings, *"It's a good thing I'm being pulled over. I'll have a good excuse for being late, and I won't have to grill pork steaks. I'll tell my wife to cancel having friends over tonight so I can relax and get over this headache."* This may be a huge stretch, but you can understand the point.

3. The third way Ted could have thought is in a neutral way that would help him feel calm or more in the middle between positive and negative. He could have thought, *"The police officer is just doing his job, and having proper lighting on a vehicle is a safety concern. I can afford to pay the fine."*

Belief Ownership Is Empowering

Belief Ownership empowers us. It is really great news to understand that we can choose how we believe, and we don't have to be victims to the events in our life. When Ted's boss tore into him, Ted would be empowered to know that what he believes about the confrontation and not what his boss says will determine how he feels.

How do you think Ted will feel if he thinks the following? *"My boss is a complete jerk. I can't believe he said that to me after the work I put into the project. It's totally unfair!"*

How might Ted feel if he chooses to think the following? *"My boss was really disappointed that the project wasn't completed on time. He has the right to be angry. I'll talk to him tomorrow about what I've done to date, and ask him for suggestions on how to help Jerry complete his part of the project. He's usually reasonable, and I'm confident that we can work through this. I don't have to get myself worked up over this."*

Beliefs Are Powerful

My favorite quote is from Henry Ford, the founder of the Ford Motor Company. He once said, "Think you can, think you can't - either way you're right." Working as a psychologist most of my life, I have found that quote to be profound. I have come to learn that our happiness and resilience is not the result of what happens to us, but is rather the consequence of how we think and respond to the events of our life.

It is possible to acquire mindsets that will help us to navigate life with confidence and courage, and there are mindsets that will cause us to live a life of fear, despair, avoidance and suffering. I will do my best to explain a way of thinking and perceiving that is rampant in our culture and many of the cultures throughout the world. Some may refer to this state of mind as being: "ego centric thinking," "mindlessness," "the false self," "defensiveness," "reactive thinking," "shallowness," and many other names. I have come up with my own name, but the name is not as important as becoming aware of a pattern of thinking that is self-limiting and at times destructive.

I believe this thinking has its roots in both our biology and what we experience and learn. I will first explain this unhealthy state of thought and then suggest a first step for managing it.

.

The Protective Child

Most people, deep down feel that they are not good enough. They long to feel important and to be recognized by others. They fear others will dislike them, embarrass them, criticize them or hurt them in some way. They are quick to place blame on others, and frequently are highly critical of themselves. They spend much of their life trying to feel "good enough" by numerous ways that ultimately are unsuccessful and lead to suffering.

When persons think and respond from their protective child mindset, they go through life wearing protective armor. Like the knights of the medieval times wore armor to protect their life, we wear a psychological armor. Unfortunately, this defensive psychological armor is worn when there is no need, and it is self-limiting and self-defeating. This defensive mindset involves insane thinking that is based on assuming, and is not based on fact.

The protective child mindset is an ineffective way of perceiving and reacting to the world with the goal of feeling important and gaining recognition. Persons using it are unaware that their pattern of thinking is based on false assumptions rather than on facts. When persons are in this mindset they see the world through the eyes of a frightened or hurt little child. They are saying through their actions, "Look at me, I'm important."

When in the protective child mindset persons are self-centered and behave in a defensive way, because they fear others will judge them as being the way they feel deep inside - as being inferior. They are unaware that their mental suffering is being caused by how they think and perceive the world. Instead they believe it is the external world and the people in it, who cause their suffering. Lashing out at others fails to resolve their feelings of inadequacy or to solve their real problems that exist in their mind.

The protective child mindset is responsible for so much of a person's ineffective thinking, feeling, and behavior. The major consequence of thinking and reacting from this ineffective mindset is that you fail to see things as they are, and you respond in irresponsible ways. Awareness is one of the most important things a person can do to escape the captivity of living life through the eyes of a frightened child filled with feelings of inadequacy. As one realizes how this ego-centric way of thinking dominates his or her life, a person can gradually choose to live life in another way.

I hope you're hanging in there with this idea of protective child mindset. The following will help you to identify your protective child when it surfaces. The story of Mike and his protective child will help you recognize some of the common patterns of thinking that underlie the protective child. If you can be more aware of your protective child, you will be empowered to choose to live your life differently and not be trapped in an attitude of victimhood.

Detecting the Protective Child Mindset

If awareness is the most effective way of freeing oneself of the protective child, what should one look for to recognize this mindset? Are there patterns of thinking and feeling that tend to point to this mindset? What actions would be indicative of a person reacting from this mindset? Let me try to demonstrate the protective child mindset with a story.

Mike and His Protective Child

Mike and Christine are awakened in the middle of the night by a phone call. Mike answers the phone and hears a male voice say, "Get your damn dogs inside, so I can get some sleep. They've been barking all night." Mike recognizes the voice as being Jeff, his next-door neighbor. Before he can think of a rational response, the caller hangs up. Mike tells Christine what happened, and he goes downstairs to the basement to check on the dogs. Just as he thought, both of his dogs are inside.

Mike opens the back door of his walk out basement, and he discovers another neighbor's little poodle has gotten her leash caught in his lilac bush and was barking. He brings the poodle inside and decides to call Julie who lives down the street. She answers and Mike says, "Julie, this is Mike. I hate to wake you, but your poodle must have gotten loose and I have her here at my place. I can keep her here until the morning, or if you want I'll turn the front light on and you can come and get her now."

Julie thanks Mike for calling, and says she'll be right over. As soon as she arrives, Mike launches into telling Julie about getting a call from Jeff. He tells her that Jeff was rude and didn't know what he was talking about when he accused Mike of leaving his dogs outside. He wraps his story up by telling Julie he'd like to give Jeff a piece of his mind and let him know how wrong he was.

After Julie leaves, Mike goes back to bed, but he can't sleep. He thinks over and over about how he had been treated unfairly by Jeff. He fantasizes about putting Jeff in his place and letting him know that he had things all wrong.

In the morning Mike voices his feelings to his wife. He retells the story of how he wants to give Jeff a piece of his mind. He goes to work and tells others at work what happened. All the while he is unaware of how his justifying thoughts are maintaining his anger. He rehearses in his mind various ways to get even with Jeff.

When he drives home he sees Jeff walking into his house. He glares at Jeff instead of giving him the usual wave. He decides to give his neighbor the silent treatment to punish him for the terrible offense he has committed. Not only does he do this for a day, but he does this for months. He holds onto this anger, and it intensifies each time he sees his neighbor.

Mike has created his own suffering by doing several things. The following are some of the reactions that reveal Mike's "protective child mindset."

Personalization was one of the first signs of his unhealthy reaction to what happened. Instead of understanding that his neighbor was frustrated by the noise of a barking dog, Mike took Jeff's rude phone call personally. He reacted as a hurt child, and became quite defensive. How often do you take things personally, when you would be better off not to?

Justification was a second sign that Mike was caught up in the protective child mindset. He told Julie about how unfairly he had been treated by Jeff's phone call. He also told the same story to his wife and the people with whom he worked. This justification helped to nurture his anger and grudge. When we are in the protective child, we strive to prove we are right and that the other person is wrong.

Rumination was the third thing that reveals the protective child mindset. When a person continues to have negative repetitive thoughts about an incident, there is a good chance that he is indulging in the protective child mindset. Our thoughts can become quite distorted, and our emotions rise when fed by the negative thinking. How much of your emotional pain involves ruminating about something that is over or something that is outside your control?

If his wife or friend were to ask Mike what's causing him to be irritable and distracted, he would likely tell the story of Jeff's phone call. **Blaming** is the fourth common sign of engaging in the protective child mindset. Mike is totally unaware that Jeff has no power over his thoughts or feelings. It is Mike himself who is choosing to attach to his hurt and angry thoughts that maintain his negative mindset. Blaming does not solve our problems and does not help us in any way.

Retaliation is one more sign that Mike was working out of the protective child. When we feel hurt, we often want to hurt the person we hold responsible for our pain. We want that person to suffer like we suffered. In his mind Mike believed he was punishing Jeff by giving him the silent treatment. Revenge is the theme of most Westerns. Getting even may be sweet in a novel or screenplay, but in real life revenge breeds more hatred and vindictiveness. It does not solve our problems, and does not bring peace of mind.

Has hatred and revenge ever solved your problems or brought happiness and peace to you? What have you successfully done in the past to leave your personal pity party, or to say good-bye to your protective child thinking? Learning to recognize the negative consequences of thinking from the protective child mindset, and having an effective game plan to stop it can enhance your psychological strength and bring you peace of mind.

Managing the Protective Child

There is a wise old saying: "A trained mind is a wonderful servant, and an untrained mind is a terrible master." I don't know the origin of this saying, but I believe it is profound. Many go through life being controlled by their thoughts that are unconsciously running through their mind. Others are aware that their thoughts are just thoughts, and they choose to select and discard various thoughts.

We have a choice in the way we choose to think about any given situation, opinion, statement, or event. Before I offer some specific strategies for taking control of our minds, I would like to address valuable information about the human brain. In chapter one I wrote about how the prefrontal cortex (PFC) is a higher functioning part of the brain from which we experience empathy and compassion and can make wise choices. I also explained that when the amygdala triggers the flight-fight-freeze reaction, that there is a hijack of the brain and we lose the ability to think clearly and wisely because we go into a protective survival mode.

In chapter four, we will discuss steps to turn off the fight-flight-freeze reaction. We will look at ways to lower stress without turning to substance use or abuse. But for now, we will focus on the basic assumptions of belief ownership. Accepting these assumptions will help you take control of your life.

Basic Assumptions of Belief Ownership

A vital step in taking control of our life, is to stop blaming others for our problems and to accept complete responsibility for how we think, feel, and act. Here are basic assumptions that can help a person move from a state of victimhood and powerlessness to a state of empowerment.

I have responsibility for and authority over my thoughts. No one has complete control of their thoughts, but we have a choice in what we think and how we think. We can choose to cling to or release various thoughts that go through our mind. We can think we will read a book, and we can choose to pick it up and start reading. We will experience distracting thoughts as we read, and we can let them take us from reading or we can return our attention to reading.

I have responsibility for and authority over my beliefs. As a child you may have been taught that what is written in a newspaper is true. You can cling to that belief, or you may choose to modify that belief based on life experiences. Many stick to beliefs that they have been taught that are not based on facts or life experience. You are responsible for what you choose to believe, and you will experience the consequences of the beliefs you hold. Many stick to self-defeating beliefs that interfere with their happiness and peace of mind. Here are a few examples. "I'm not worthy." "I'm not smart enough." "I'm a bad person."

I have responsibility for and authority over my feelings. An emotion involves a physical response to a prompting event. I might smile if given an ice cream cone, or I might experience a racing heart and tremble if a vicious dog growls and approaches me. Those two prompting events are external. I might also cry when thinking about a loved family member who recently died, or I might laugh thinking about something funny my two-year-old grandson said. Those are examples of internal prompting events. Way too often we blame others for our feelings. We cannot control our feelings, but we need to take responsibility for them. How we choose to think and what we choose to do when we experience feelings lends us a good deal of control of them.

I have responsibility for and authority over my desires and urges. I might have the thought, "I'd love to have a peanut butter chocolate shake topped with whip cream and a cherry." I may hop in my car and get that milkshake. If I weigh 300 pounds as a result of giving into my urges, it makes no sense to blame my parents for giving me a "fat" gene or for giving me milkshakes as a child. It helps me in no way to blame my boss for stressing me out and contributing to my emotional eating. When I accept responsibility for my desires and urges, then and only then can I take action to control those urges. At that point, I might do research that helps me understand what types of foods are most addictive, and what I need to do to start breaking those addictive eating patterns.

I have responsibility for and authority over my actions. A person might say something to me that is insulting and hurtful. I may automatically react in a defensive manner and say something insulting in return. I may stuff my hurt feelings and hold onto them. I may assertively approach the person, and request that he not repeat that behavior in the future. I alone am responsible for my actions, and I will experience the consequences of how I react or respond in any given situation. Choosing to respond mindfully can free us from much conflict and feelings of guilt and shame. Most importantly, we need to accept responsibility for the actions we take, and it is often hurtful to our self-esteem and our relationships when we blame others for our behavior.

Activities to Build Psychological Strength

1. Stop blaming others and yourself. Accept full responsibility for your actions. If you make a mistake or do something that is ineffective, simply respond by saying things like: "I messed up." "I made a mistake." "My intent wasn't to hurt you, and I'm sorry."

2. Become aware that in a given situation you can choose to have positive, negative or neutral thoughts. Since your emotions, to a large degree, flow from your thoughts, - work on having less negative thoughts. Strive to see things as they really are, and avoid making things much better or much worse than how they actually are.

3. Become aware of how your actions and thinking frequently come out of a protective child

mindset. Observe when you're feeling not good enough, or find it necessary to defend your ego. Let go of your ego and respond in a mindful way.

4. **Become aware that others may be thinking from their protective child mindset.** Try to feel compassion for others who become defensive, and realize they may be struggling with a deeply held belief that they are not good enough. Develop compassion for others and yourself as you accept that life is, at times, quite difficult.

5. **Strive to not take things so personally.** In place of thinking hurt and angry thoughts, adopt a state of being curious. What are some reasons why the person offending you said or did what they did? Why did their actions trigger your negative feelings? Could there be something else going on?

6. **Make a consistent effort to speak in a way where you are taking full responsibility for how you think, feel and act.** Make certain that your words and actions demonstrate that you are assuming responsibility. "I'm feeling depressed due to not getting enough exercise and forgetting to be grateful." “I'm angry because I've been ruminating about the police officer giving me a driving ticket.” "I feel happy because I went for a walk and focused on the sunshine and beautiful scenery."

7. **Pay attention to how you feel differently when you own your thoughts and feelings.** Pay attention to how others respond to you. Realize that at first it will feel strange to you simply because it’s new. It will likely feel strange to others around you, because it’s new. Just because it’s new and feels strange doesn’t mean it’s wrong or that it won't help.

Chapter 3: Belief Management

Getting Unstuck from the Mud

SECRET: Understanding the power of your thoughts and developing belief management skills can radically improve your life.

I'm happy that you are continuing to read and develop psychological strength. In chapter one, you learned about the importance of taking care of your body, because it helps your mind to think more clearly and allows you to be less stressed. In chapter two, you learned that accepting full responsibility for your thoughts, feelings and actions will free you from being a victim, and will empower you to live life with more meaning and happiness.

In this chapter you will learn a technique to recognize unhealthy beliefs, and will be shown strategies and skills to change those self-defeating beliefs. So many people spend much of their life worrying about things outside their control. That worry robs them of finding peace and happiness in the present moment. Others are stuck brooding about things that have happened to them in the past that they cannot change. I believe this chapter will help you to take more control over your mind and your life.

Getting Stuck in the Mud

When I was a young man, in my twenties, I had a friend who agreed to help me get some firewood for Bud, my father-in-law. Jim's family owned some timber land off a country road. Bud loaned me his small pickup truck, and Jim and I drove out to his family's wooded land on a nice fall day. Jim did most of the cutting with the chainsaw, and I did most of the loading onto my father-in-law's truck. I chose to do the manual work, because I wanted to return home with the same ten fingers I had when I arrived at the site.

At one point we decided we had a load, and I started the truck. The ground was soft from a recent rain, and the back tires started digging into the soft ground with the weight of the load of wood. Jim suggested that we walk to the nearest farmhouse and see if someone might give us a tow. The man of the house was willing to help, but before we left I called home. I let my wife know what had happened and that we would be late. I also spoke to Bud. Fortunately, he didn't sound angry, but he did ask directions as to where we were.

Soon we were back at the small truck that was stuck in the mud. The good Samaritan tied a tow rope securely to the small pickup, and he attached the other end to the bumper hitch of his big truck. As he applied the gas, his back tires dug deeper and deeper into the mud. He kept putting the pedal to the metal until his truck was buried to the axle. Now we had two trucks stuck, and the smaller pickup was only two or three inches deep in the mud. While the farmer went back to his house to call a professional tow truck, my father-in-law arrived.

Bud parked his car and took the keys to his truck. He rocked it back and forth from low to reverse and back using the manual gear shift, and soon drove the little truck out of the woods to the solid country road.

The helpful farmer's belief that he could muscle the little truck out by stepping harder on the gas pedal had failed. Likewise, in life, we often cling to irrational and faulty beliefs that cause us to feel worse and worse, and to stay stuck in a pattern of behavior that is self-defeating. Unless you learn to manage your beliefs, you may find yourself frequently stuck in the ruts of life. This chapter will give you several different skills to help you first identify unhealthy and ineffective beliefs and then change those beliefs.

Belief Management Defined

Belief Management is defined in two parts: 1) *the awareness that the way one chooses to think or believe greatly affects one's emotional state and behavior, and 2) the ability to identify and change ineffective thoughts and beliefs to more effective patterns of thinking will improve one's emotional state and ability to accomplish life goals.* Although this rather complex definition at first glance may be confusing, you will in time discover that a clear understanding and mastery of belief management can help you radically change your life.

The Story of Barb

Barb is a young woman in her early 30's who woke up in a good mood until she found a lump in her left breast during her morning shower. Unfortunately, Barb had poor belief management skills. Her emotions quickly changed from happiness to anxiety and depression. She drove to her job in the city, but her worry about having cancer made it difficult for her to focus on her work. She also failed to show the bubbly personality for which she was known. By the end of the day, she had convinced herself that she had breast cancer and would die like her aunt Betty died two years earlier. Barb had unintentionally allowed her negative thinking to both scare her and cause her to be depressed.

The good news is that two weeks later Barb's physician informed her that the lump was a noncancerous cyst. The bad news is that for those two weeks Barb's faulty belief had made her extremely miserable. However, if you asked Barb what had made her miserable, she would show no awareness that she was responsible for her misery. She would explain that the lump in her breast had been the culprit that had caused her anxiety and depression. In reality it was Barb's faulty belief that she had cancer that created her psychological downslide. Barb could have avoided her extreme negative mood had she realized she could have changed her belief and taken effective steps to do so.

3 Rational Questions

This lesson will teach you how to determine if a thought or belief is rational or irrational. You will also learn specific skills to help you change ineffective beliefs to more rational beliefs. In his workbook, *A Client's Guide to Cognitive Behavior Therapy,* Aldo Pucci teaches 3 questions you can ask yourself to determine if a belief is rational or irrational. He refers to these questions as the 3 Rational Questions.

Here are the 3 rational questions:

1. **Is this belief based on facts?**
2. **Does this belief help me to achieve my goals?**
3. **Does this belief help me to feel the way I want to feel?**

He explains that if you answer "no" to any one of the 3 questions, then the belief is an irrational belief for you.

If Barb had asked the ***Three Rational Questions***, she would have quickly determined that the belief she had cancer and would die soon was an irrational belief. Let's quickly examine the questions.

1. Is this belief factual? No! Barb had no factual evidence that she had cancer. Even if the lump had been cancerous, there would have been various options for medically treating it.

2. Does this belief help Barb to achieve her goals? No! For those two weeks, Barb's belief that she had cancer greatly interfered with her accomplishing her goals.

3. Does this belief help Barb to feel the way she wanted to feel? No! It prevented her from feeling peace of mind and happiness, and instead caused her to feel frightened and depressed.

If the answer to any of the 3 questions is no, then the person can have confidence that the thought is ineffective. This is important, but even of greater importance is having a method of refuting the negative belief that can rob one of peace of mind.

3 Rational Steps to Change Negative Beliefs

There are some simple steps one can use to change an identified negative belief. Here are my three favorites.

1. Label the belief as "Hurtful and not factually true." In the story about Barb, it would have been helpful for Barb to have told herself, "This belief that I have cancer and I'm dying is hurtful and not factually true." Some of my clients prefer to label their irrational beliefs as " bullshit thinking".

2. Replace the irrational or ineffective belief with a more rational and effective belief. Barb could change the belief to, "I have a lump in my breast, and I will see a doctor to determine if there is an issue needing treatment or not."

3. Write the replacement belief on an index card and refer to it often until the irrational thought slowly fades away and the new belief takes its place.

Exterminating the ANTS

Daniel Amen is a noted psychiatrist and author. In some of his books he talks about taking action to exterminate the ***automatic negative thoughts (ANTS)*** that rob persons of happiness and prevent them from living a more meaningful life. In his book, *Use Your Brain to Change Your Age*, Dr. Amen lists the following four questions to help persons challenge their automatic negative thoughts. Carefully, read through these four questions.

1. Is what I'm thinking true?

2. Can I absolutely know it is true?

3. How do I react when I believe that thought?

4. Who would I be without the thought? Or, put differently, how would I feel if I didn't have the thought?

I would encourage you to take a piece of paper out now and write down a negative automatic thought you have that is hurtful to your happiness, confidence, or productivity. Then write your response to each of Dr. Amen's four ANT killer questions.

I strongly urge you to use the 3 Rational Questions to determine if certain beliefs are rational or not. Realize that most of the time when you experience intense negative emotions, there are irrational thoughts and beliefs fueling those strong feelings. Identifying ineffective beliefs and replacing them with more rational and effective beliefs will make a huge difference in your level of psychological strength.

The ***3 Rational Questions*** and the ***ANT Eater Questions*** have helped numerous persons to refute negative beliefs that have caused emotional pain and hindered them from living a full and productive life. But there are often times when a person who is experiencing intense negative feelings is unable to respond intelligently. Why is this?

Turning Off the Fight-Flight Reaction

You may need to take steps to relax your body and calm your mind before using cognitive skills to change your irrational beliefs. During the discussion of the STOP Skill in chapter one, you were made aware that when a person is highly anxious or engaged in intense negative emotions, he is probably in a survival mode - often referred to as the fight-flight-freeze reaction. During this physiological response the higher functioning portion of the brain is hijacked by a more primitive portion. In those situations, there is a disconnect with the prefrontal cortex (PFC). The PFC is a higher functioning part of the brain that allows one to have empathy and compassion for others and make wise decisions.

When a person is in survival mode, adrenalin and the stress hormone cortisol are released into the blood stream. Adrenalin speeds up respiration and heart rate to prepare the body to fight or flee. Cortisol triggers hyper-vigilance that increases irritability and makes it difficult to sleep.

How to Turn on the Relaxation Response

There are three activities that have proven effective in turning on the relaxation response and decreasing cortisol levels. The first activity is **exercise**. Intense exercise allows a person to expend energy and calm the body down after the exercise is completed. The second activity is **slow, deep breathing**. I often help clients calm down when they are highly anxious by having them breathe in through their nose slowly for 6 to 8 seconds, and breathe out through their mouth for the same amount of time. The third activity is **meditation**. A simple meditation is to breathe in slowly through the nose while saying to oneself, "As I breathe in I feel calm." Then to breathe out slowly through the mouth and say, "As I breathe out I release stress." Continue to do this for five minutes.

I would encourage anyone who is serious about better managing their beliefs and emotions to start getting some routine exercise, preferably in a way they enjoy. Doing slow, deep breathing for three minutes, three times a day will have a positive effect on your psychological strength. More and more research, show numerous health and psychological benefits of meditation. There are numerous You Tube videos on the topic of meditation. Do some research.

Big Box Vs. Little Box

In chapter one I encouraged you to write down what was out of your control and what was in your control. I made that idea into a handout about twenty years ago. It is the handout that I have given more clients than any other, and I call it the Big Box vs. Little Box. At the top of the page is printed "Out of My Control." In a small box in the middle of the page is printed "In My Control." Clients are encouraged to write or at least mentally identify many things that are disturbing them that are outside of their control. I encourage them to let go of those things they cannot control or influence. They soon discover that they cannot change others, and the only thing they really have control over is how they respond to others and the situations that arise in their life.

On the back of the handout are two opposing ways of thinking. One has seven beliefs of victimhood. The second has seven beliefs of empowerment. When persons take responsibility for the choices they make they grow in empowerment. The state of victimhood is extremely self-destructive. It involves self-pity, blaming, and ruminating thoughts that keep one stuck in a negative state of feeling. The simple step of recognizing and letting go of things out of one's control can be powerful and enable you to better manage your thoughts and feelings.

Acceptance of Reality Lessens Suffering

Accepting reality is a life changer. In chapter two the protective-child state was discussed. In that mindset persons often misperceive reality, and look at the world through the eyes of a hurt and frightened child. There is an ongoing belief that things should be as the person wants things to be and not as they are. This leads to intense frustration and outer conflict with others.

Accepting reality does not require one to like reality or to do nothing to create positive change. It is simply accepting the reality that things are as they are. Imagine a couple has planned to have a picnic at a beautiful park on the second Sunday of May. When they wake up that Sunday, it is pouring rain and the weather forecaster announces it is to rain all day. Non-acceptance of reality would sound like this. "It's not fair. Earlier this week the weatherman said it would be sunny on Sunday. I made potato salad, and we have burgers to cook. This was supposed to be a wonderful day for a picnic."

On the other hand, acceptance sounds like this. "It's raining and the forecast predicts rain throughout the day. Let's catch a movie, and later I'll grill the hamburgers on the indoor grill and we'll have our picnic at home." Acceptance of reality can lead to positive coping, while non-acceptance pulls persons into emotional suffering.

Persons may go through their entire life holding onto memories of something their mom or dad did to them as a child that they have judged to be unfair or terribly wrong. They talk about the same incident over and over when they are around other family members. Their voice intensifies as they explain how they were wronged, and how it has limited their ability to experience peace and happiness. ***They do not understand that their attachment to the memory and their rumination about the event, and not the event itself, has caused them most of the suffering.***

Many hold onto unrealistic expectations for their parents, their spouse or partner, or someone else of importance in their life. They have a faulty belief that they can change the person in question. When they try to change the other person and that person doesn't change, they become highly frustrated and may fall into a state of despair. It would be much more effective to accept the reality that the person is the way they are, and it is unlikely they will change. This acceptance frees them to set healthy boundaries and to live their life without trying to change someone they have no control over.

Can't Change It

In his bestselling book, *The Miracle Morning*, Hal Elrod tells the story of how the words "can't change it" changed his life. At age twenty, Hal was in a horrific car accident when he was struck by a pickup head on that was going the wrong way down the freeway. His heart stopped and he almost bled to death after being removed from his car. He was rushed by helicopter to the hospital and doctors were able to save his life, but they told his parents that Hal may never walk again, and there was a possibility he might not awaken from the coma.

When Hal did awaken from the coma six days later, it was not long before he was smiling and laughing with staff. After this unexpected pattern of positivity went on for days, the medical staff were concerned that Hal was in denial and urged his parents to talk to him about the reality of his situation. When his father spoke to his son, Hal explained that he had learned to live by the ***five-minute rule.*** The five-minute rule that his mentor taught him in sales was - it was okay to experience feelings of disappointment or anger when something went wrong, but it was best to understand that if one cannot change what has happened that after five minutes they need to fully accept it and move on with their life.

Hal told his dad that he accepted that it was a possibility he may never walk again, and if that turned out to be a reality - he would strive to be one of the happiest persons in a wheelchair. However, he was planning to do everything within his ability to walk again. Not only did Hal in time walk again. In several years he ran an ultra-marathon of just over 52 miles.

How might your life be different, if you used the words "can't change it" to accept mistakes or disappointments and to move on with your life? What are some things that have happened to you in the past that you still think about often and feel hurt, resentment and anger? Persons who accept reality and let go of their negative thoughts and emotions show psychological strength and will experience more peace of mind.

I would like you to try some of the different belief management skills discussed in this chapter. Please pay attention to how your thoughts impact your feelings and actions. How might your life be different, if you learn skills to stop your negative and ineffective thinking? How might it be different if you started tackling those things that you now avoid due to your anxiety and fear? Using these belief management skills will help you to become a more resilient person.

Please select one activity to focus on. Do it consistently long enough to see if it is working for you. Circle the number in front of it to show you have completed it. Then go to another activity and do the same.

Activities to Build Psychological Strength

1. Pay attention to when you are having negative emotions, and check how your thoughts and beliefs contribute to that emotion. Realize that you may experience more control of your life when you change and refute negative and irrational beliefs. We have limited control over what happens to us, but we have total responsibility for how we respond.

2. Use the 3 Rational Questions to help identify irrational beliefs. The questions are: 1. Is this belief based on fact? 2. Does this belief help me to reach my goals? 3. Does this belief help me to feel the way I want to feel? It the answer to any of these three questions is no, then the belief is irrational or ineffective.

3. Once identified, label the negative belief and replace it with a healthier belief. Label the negative belief as untrue and hurtful. Then replace it with a more rational and healthy belief.

4. Use Dr. Daniel Amen's four ANT Killer Questions. 1. Is what I'm thinking true? 2. Can I absolutely know it is true? 3. How do I react when I believe that thought? 4. Who would I be without the thought? Or, put differently, how would I feel if I didn't have the thought?

5. Turn off the fight-flight-freeze reaction. Participate in some type of routine exercise. Most adults would benefit from 150 minutes of exercise weekly. Take slow and deep breaths for three minutes three times a day. Make some time each day for meditation in which you relax your body and quiet your mind.

6. Let go of things out of your control. Worry and anxiety can be significantly decreased by paying attention to those things we worry about that are outside our control and then letting go of them.

7. Stop ruminating when you CAN'T CHANGE IT. As soon as you understand that you can't change something, accept that it is over and stop devoting time to it. When you accept you can't change it, then you are free to focus your attention on things you have some control over.

Chapter 4: Taking the Middle Path

Driving Down the Center of Your Lane

SECRET: Recognizing and taking the middle path can enhance your life and free you from the consequences of rigid thinking and overreacting.

After reading chapter three, you have skills to identify and change your irrational beliefs. This should help you lessen your worry and anxiety. It is time now to enhance your psychological strength by teaching you other mindful ways of thinking and acting.

I have written chapter four to help you approach life with an open mind. Many experience conflict and anger as a result of their judgmental and rigid thinking. I want you to avoid getting caught up with trying to prove you're right. Instead, I'd like you to be free to experience more peace of mind and happiness

In this chapter I will teach you how to develop the courage to be imperfect. You will also be helped to understand that you cannot please everyone, and that it is important to stick to your values and be yourself. I will also explain that forgiveness is something you do for yourself, and that it can be a powerful tool for releasing anger and bitterness related to past hurts.

Approaching Life with an Open Mind

I believe being open-minded about life is a gift. All too often persons are burdened with rigid beliefs and are quick to judge and blame. This prevents them from learning to see things through the eyes of another. It creates more conflict and leads to self-condemnation.

I enjoy spending time with people who have an open mind. I feel comfortable in their presence, because I have no need to fear that they are going to judge me and put me down. Open-minded people tend to be happier and more positive due to their approach to life. Sometimes they show a wonderful curiosity that propels them to learn more and more about life and others.

Problems with Rigid Thinking

As a child we were likely taught to think in all or nothing ways for our survival. It is wise to not touch a hot frying pan, to always look both ways before entering a busy street, and to fasten our seat belt. As a young child we believe what our parents tell us, because we have not yet developed critical thinking.

When I was probably three or four, I noticed that the rising moon appeared yellow as it lifted up over the horizon. I asked my dad, "Why is the moon yellow?" He responded, "Because it's made of green cheese." At that time, I believed the moon must have been made out of green cheese, because that is what Dad told me. However, I wondered why it looked yellow and not green.

Unfortunately, we may learn many things from our parents, caregivers or others as a child that are completely untrue. For instance, I learned from certain TV westerns that the American Indians were savages that hunted and scalped the white man. As an adult I learned that my ancestors were at times savages that took the land from the American Indians who had lived there for centuries before the European settlers came to America. Because they had superior weapons, they were able to prevail when it came to battles.

When we think rigidly, we believe we are right and the other person is wrong. It becomes so easy to judge others, and to fail to see the common link we have with others. It is easy to label someone as a drug addict, instead of seeing a person who is struggling is more like us than different from us. It is also easy to block out our own addictions from our mind, and to think, "I'm not a drug addict." At the same time, we may be an emotional eater, a compulsive spender, a couch potato, or whatever dysfunctional pattern of behavior we have. We are more likely to treat the person we labeled as a drug addict with a lack of respect, because we have labeled them as "bad" in our minds.

Rigid thinking prevents us from learning. If we believe whatever we think is right, there is no need to learn to think any differently. We are not open to new ideas that could be helpful to us. Have you ever found yourself closed to an idea that you later found to be helpful to you?

Staying in the Center of Your Lane

There are times when I'm driving and I happen onto road construction over a highway bridge. On my left are huge concrete barriers, and on my right are oncoming traffic. At those times, I feel anxiety because I know if I turn slightly to my left I will strike the concrete barrier or slightly to the right I will hit oncoming traffic. At those times, I carefully focus on driving down the center of my lane.

In life we often feel better and do better when we take the middle path. For instance, when dining at a restaurant we may have ordered a steak well done. After our waitress delivers it and we slice into it, we may find it rare and not suitable for our taste. On one extreme, we could become angry and talk rudely to the waitress blaming her for something outside her control. On the other extreme, we could say nothing and leave the steak uneaten. If we do this, we will likely feel upset with the restaurant and dissatisfied when we leave. The middle path would be to show the steak to the waitress, and politely ask her to have it cooked the way it was ordered.

Life becomes easier when we learn to take the middle path. It is helpful to be able to see things from another's point of view and from our own. There are times to compromise and times when it is wise to not. Let's explore the idea of dialectical thinking.

Dialectical Thinking

Dialectical thinking involves finding a middle path or synthesis between two opposing thoughts. In life there are many times when we can hold two opposing thoughts to be true. I can be angry at my grandson for tracking mud on my carpet, and love him at the same time. I can be grateful that the mechanic fixed my transmission and at the same time be unhappy that the bill for the repair was much higher than I anticipated.

Dialectical thinking involves learning to avoid judgmental thinking, and to become aware of how our judgments intensify our negative feelings. Let's compare how Jessica is to likely feel and respond when she thinks judgmentally versus thinking dialectically. Jessica asked Robby, her husband, to load the dishwasher and pick up the kitchen while she goes grocery shopping so she can start dinner when she gets home.

In scenario one, Jessica comes home and finds that Robby is talking on the phone to his brother and has done very little work on the kitchen. She glares at him and when he finishes the phone call, she says, "You haven't done anything to the kitchen. I asked you to do a few simple things so I could fix dinner, and you chose to ignore me and talk to your brother. Just get out of my way, and I'll clean the kitchen and fix dinner while you sit on your ass!" You can see that her judgments intensified her feelings of anger, and is unlikely to find a resolution to the conflict.

In scenario two, Jessica again comes home and finds Robby is talking on the phone to his brother and has done very little work on the kitchen. She has learned to think in a dialectical and non-judgmental way. She starts putting the groceries away and Robby comes in and says, "I'm sorry I didn't get the kitchen picked up. Jimmy has been having a rough time at work and is thinking about looking for another job." Jessica listens and carries on a conversation as they put the groceries away. When they finish with the groceries, Jessica says, "I'd like it if you took me out to eat tonight, because I don't feel like cleaning the kitchen and then cooking." Robby agrees to do this, and both of them enjoy eating Mexican food. Neither is angry with the other.

What Stands in the Way of Dialectical Thinking?

A major obstacle to dialectical thinking is that ***we all have a bias of seeing things from our viewpoint***. In the first scenario, when Jessica came home, she could only see that her husband had failed to meet her request. She got stuck thinking about how unfair it was, and how it would make things more difficult for her. In the second, she tended to simply see that her husband was talking on the phone to his brother and had not picked up the kitchen. She did not judge him for it, and instead waited to find out what he had to say.

A second obstacle to keeping an open mind and thinking dialectically is that ***we allow our emotions to take control of our thoughts and actions***. When we engage in intense feelings we often fall into the fight-flight reaction. Our thinking becomes clouded because we have a disconnect with the higher functioning prefrontal cortex of the brain. In scenario one, Jessica became quite angry. Soon she was acting out of anger, and she was no longer able to see a multitude of possible solutions to the problem. In fact, she punished herself by being a martyr and cleaning the kitchen and fixing dinner. Her intent was to make Robby feel guilty, but Robby has a choice as to how he thinks and feels.

A third roadblock to dialectical thought is that ***we may have learned ineffective patterns of responding that need to be unlearned before we can do something differently***. It is quite possible that Jessica learned to be blaming and angry from her mom or dad. They may have used guilt trips on each other or on Jessica. Without awareness Jessica can continue in the same pattern of rigid thinking and ineffective behavior. Failure to identify and correct ineffective patterns of responding may prevent a person from learning to think dialectically and from responding mindfully.

Responding Non-Judgmentally

Take a moment to reflect on what happens when you become judgmental. Do you feel self-righteous? Do you use colorful language? Do you justify or give reasons to support you are right and the other person is wrong? Does the intensity of your negative emotions rise? I want you to understand that learning to be less judgmental can free you from much of your anger and resentment.

Often judgment refers to labeling someone or something as being good or bad. If my next-door neighbor talks about being a compulsive shoplifter, it would be prudent to not go shopping with him. In a non-judgmental way, I can think, "I wouldn't feel comfortable shopping with Charles, because he told me he shoplifts." This is quite different than thinking, "Charles is an idiot and a thief."

Charles is not just a shoplifter. He is a person and there are reasons why he shoplifts that I may never understand. If I judge him and treat him like he is worthless, then I am disrespecting him. If I treat him with respect, I may find that he has many positive qualities, and I may possibly be a positive influence in his life and he in mine.

One of the first things we can do to become less judgmental, is to pay attention to how often we make judgments. We also need to show awareness of how those judgments affect our mood and actions. Some persons may get a counter, and click it each time they are judgmental. Monitoring our judgments usually tends to cause them to decrease.

A second step, in curbing our judgments is to pay attention to our "should thinking." There is a saying that when I should on others - I get angry at them, and when I should on me - I get angry at myself. I have encouraged many of my clients to substitute the four words "it would be nice" for "should." I will feel differently if I think it would have been nice if my wife did the dishes, as compared to thinking my wife should have done the dishes. Simply notice how you become angrier at others or feel guilty yourself when you employ should thinking.

Being Non-Judgmental and Sticking to Values

Some people think that being non-judgmental means discarding your values. Values are quite important, and being non-judgmental does not mean you are throwing them away. I believe being honest and truthful is both healthy and wise. At the same time, I may have compassion for someone who lies, and realize that lying typically grows out of fear.

I have experienced that judgments often come out of the protective child mindset discussed earlier in this book. Because we feel we are not good enough, we often try to feel better by judging others as "bad" to help us feel "good." When we try to build ourselves up by putting others down, we end up creating conflict and feel worse ourselves. The best way to feel better about yourself, is to strive to encourage and build others up around you. Encouragement is a win-win for you and the other person.

The Courage to Be Imperfect

In our culture there is strong push to be our best and to strive for perfection. We also tend to feel shame when we make a mistake, or fail to do things to the best of our ability. You have probably heard the expression, paralysis by analysis. There is paralysis caused by the fear of failing to be perfect.

The antidote to perfectionism is the courage to be imperfect. I have learned that it is okay to make mistakes, and when I am able to laugh at myself I become psychologically stronger. I have respect for persons who are able to laugh at themselves, and who have stopped trying to project an image of being perfect. Making mistakes is a part of life, and the wise person is able to face his or her mistakes and to learn from them.

There was a day that I had dressed in the dark so I wouldn't disturb my sleeping wife. A couple hours later I was seeing a client in my office and crossed my leg over my knee. I glanced down at my brown shoe and thought "that's funny I thought I wore my black shoes." I looked down at my other foot and observed that I was wearing one black shoe and one brown shoe.

Before I had developed some courage to be imperfect, I would have been very self-conscious and fearful that others would see me and think I was stupid for wearing one black and one brown shoe. I would have snuck out of my office at lunchtime and driven 20 minutes home to change shoes and 20 minutes back to my office. Instead, I went out after my session and asked the receptionist how she liked my shoes. We both laughed and I explained that I had two almost identical pairs of shoes, except one pair was brown and the other black. At lunch, I walked bravely over to the cafeteria prepared to laugh at my mistake, but I don't think a single person even looked at my shoes.

The middle path is one of striving to do quality work without being obsessed with perfectionism. It is okay to take pride in our work, but we don't need to be living in fear of making a mistake. When one does make a mistake, then be honest and take responsibility for the mistake instead of trying to cover it up. Persons who do this are usually more respected by others than the one who pretends to be something he or she is not - perfect.

Don't Be Too Big of a Pleaser

Closely linked to perfectionism is the fear of disappointing others. Persons often get caught up in trying to make everyone happy with their actions. It has been my experience that the harder one tries to please others the more others expect and demand to be pleased.

If mom tries to be overly fair with her kids, then she will buy young Billy a new pair of shoes because she bought a new pair for Jessica, his older sister. By repeating this pattern of always getting something for one child that she gets for the other, the daughter and son soon learn to expect something if their sibling gets something. If Jessica out grows her coat, it makes no sense to buy a new coat for Billy when his jacket fits and is in good shape. However, Billy will likely throw a fit if mom doesn't get something for him. What do you think mom will likely do if she feels she must please her children all the time?

Adult children may strive to always make their mom or dad happy with them if they have become pleasers. Persons who are pleasers often fail to speak up for themselves, and often feel resentful because others do not sacrifice for them like they sacrifice for others. Persons can become paralyzed with the fear that if they do something important for themselves, then someone else may become upset or angry with them. This communicates to the other person "guilt trips work really well on me - go ahead and take advantage of me."

There are times that pleasing others can be a win-win situation. It is okay to enjoy doing things for others, and to enjoy seeing them feel happy and pleased. It is not okay to go through life living in fear of disappointing someone. Some people become "compulsive pleasers" because they were hurt by others who became hostile and critical when they didn't get their way. Others grew up with someone who was a "compulsive pleaser" and therefore believed that was the thing to do. Some persons become "compulsive pleasers" because they were taught that a good person always puts others first.

I like to please others, but not to the extent that I allow others to take advantage of me. I have learned that I am a happier person when I walk the middle path of being caring without neglecting myself. I do my best to avoid being a martyr. It never made me feel good when someone sacrificed for me and then slapped me with a giant guilt trip. In some ways I have learned that resentment is not a healthy emotion for me to experience, and I try my best to avoid it.

Forgiveness Is a Middle Path

Working as a therapist, I have encountered many clients who have been consumed with feelings of bitterness, rage and hatred. I have learned of horrific acts that one person has inflicted on another.

Some persons find it so difficult to forgive, that they never experience the letting go of suffering that comes with it. Others discover considerable peace and have been able to move forward with life through forgiving the person or persons who have traumatized them or gravely hurt them.

How can forgiving someone be a middle path? Isn't forgiveness an extreme measure? Is it impossible to forgive someone when they have brutally abused you? I view forgiveness to be a healthy middle path between the extremes of pretending that the wrongful action never happened and holding onto the belief that I have been profoundly injured and must exact revenge on the offending person to find peace of mind.

Why Is It Difficult to Forgive?

I believe there are a number of different reasons why it is difficult to forgive. Some have grown up in an environment where family members did not forgive one another, and dealt with hurt by trying to exact revenge. Others see forgiveness as something that "Bible thumpers" say you should do. Some believe that justice means getting even. Others may believe that forgiveness means that the abusive action was right or that I need to allow abuse to continue.

Forgiveness is something that a person does for oneself. It allows the person to stop ruminating about the past that cannot be changed. It frees the person to live more in the present moment. It makes room for the person to experience positive emotions, which are difficult to feel when one is obsessing about a hurtful experience or is plotting revenge.

Forgiving someone does not mean that what the person did was okay, or that we will allow abuse to continue. If a friend borrows a $100 and promises to pay it back on payday and doesn't pay it back, it makes sense to assertively ask for the money. If after repeated attempts the friend does not pay the money back, one can forgive and decide to end the relationship or continue the relationship with the understanding not to lend money again. Forgiveness is accepting the reality that the person is unwilling to pay the money back. It is also letting go of the ruminating thoughts about the unfairness that serve to maintain feelings of betrayal and anger.

What Are Steps of Forgiving?

1. Be honest about what happened. Be honest with yourself about what happened and what you feel.

2. Try to look at things through the eyes of the offending party. All of us are biased by our perception, which often is inaccurate. Try to understand why the person did what they did that wronged you.

3. Understand that hurtful behavior often comes out of human weakness. Did the person act in a hurtful way because they were intoxicated? Were they defending their ego? Were they highly stressed and unable to think clearly?

4. Process your own hurt or anger. It is often helpful for a person to write a "no send letter" to express how they think and feel about what happened. Usually it is best to not send the letter to the offending party.

5. Plan out what you need to do. Do you need to burn the letter you've written? Do you need to assertively talk to the person and let them know what you request, and what you will do if they do not honor your request?

6. Decide to forgive - to have peace of mind. Make the decision to let go so you will not have to carry those angry thoughts and painful emotions around.

7. Let go, and if needed, wish the offending person well or pray for the person. Forgiveness is a process that may take time and repeated efforts to let go of the past.

I would like to share a poem I wrote on forgiving. It conveys my thoughts on how forgiveness is a choice to end our mental suffering and to move on with life. I trust that you will see the benefit of nurturing a forgiving mind and heart.

Forgiving

Forgiving is a choice I make to heal
emotional pain,
And it is not an invitation for others
to take advantage of me.
As long as I choose to fill my mind with
thoughts of vindictiveness,
I have given you control of my mind
and heart.
I forgive you because I no longer want
to give you a place in my heart,
For I want to have ample space in it to
experience joy and love.
I forgive you because I choose to enjoy
peace of mind,
And I cannot do so as long as I entertain
thoughts of getting even.
Often the actual wrongful action of
another is momentary,
But the holding onto can last for eternity
if we allow it.
I wish you well and hope that you will
grow to be a healthier person,
And in my forgiving you, I choose to live
in the present and not the past.
I can choose nothing other than to
forgive you,
For I care too much for myself to
not let go.

Activities to Build Psychological Strength

1. Be open-minded. Approach life with an open mind and be curious as to how and why others think and believe the way they do. Value diversity.

2. Try to understand the viewpoint of others. Respect that everyone has the right to believe the way they do, even though you may view things differently.

3. Look for the middle path. Often the middle path is a wise place to be. As you try to understand extreme points of view, look for the path that makes the most sense.

4. Strive to be non-judgmental. Remember that judgments often intensify our negative feelings and lead to conflict. Practice being less judgmental.

5. Develop the courage to be imperfect. Show the courage to admit your mistakes. Discover peace of mind by letting go of perfectionism. Learn to laugh at your mistakes and to learn from them.

6. Stop trying to please everyone. Do what you believe is right, and understand that often in life others may not agree with us. We can create enormous anxiety when we try to please everyone.

7. Learn to forgive and let go of bitterness. Realize that forgiveness is something that benefits oneself. It enables us to let go of hurt, anger and bitterness. Forgiveness makes more room for us to enjoy life.

Chapter 5: Overcoming Procrastination

Becoming a Better Driver

SECRET: Procrastination can be conquered by focusing on doing more of one positive activity and doing less of one non-productive activity long enough for both to become habits.

I am writing this chapter, because I realize you probably struggle with finishing many of your important activities in a timely manner. It is difficult, if not impossible, to lead a productive and fulfilling life without taking steps to reduce procrastination. At the same time, you need to be careful not to become overly compulsive and rigid in achieving goals. As you learned in chapter four, it is wise to take a middle path that brings balance to your life.

In chapter five, I will explain what procrastination is and why so many people fall victim to it. I will teach you about the power of reinforcement - both positive and negative. Then I will encourage you to develop a meaningful morning routine to start your day off right.

Before completing this chapter, you will learn how to write effective goals. I will explain how willpower is finite, and how to use this limited resource in an effective manner. Most importantly of all, I will give you a simple strategy for replacing bad habits with good habits - the key for conquering procrastination.

What Is Procrastination?

Procrastination is playing my favorite video game when I planned to be writing. It is watching TV when I told my wife I would mow the yard. It is eating chips and salsa when I need to be making a phone call. ***Procrastination is avoiding doing something that is unpleasant or difficult that needs to be done, and instead doing something that is comforting or anxiety reducing.***

Almost all people procrastinate. Some excel at putting things off, while others exhibit a higher level of self-discipline and are more productive. The consequences of frequent procrastination include reduced accomplishment, lowered self-esteem, guilt feelings, and conflict with persons harmed or disappointed by one's failure to keep commitments.

How will your life be different, if you learn to overcome procrastination? What things will you will accomplish, if you stop avoiding them? How will you feel about yourself, if you develop a pattern of getting things done in a timely manner? How will people who care about you respond, if you show major improvement in fulfilling your responsibilities?

Becoming a Better Driver

To become a better driver there are two essential things that any driver needs to do. The first is to decrease or completely stop bad driving habits. The second is to develop or increase good driving habits. Would you be a better driver if you decreased bad driving habits, such as, talking on your cell while driving through busy traffic, eating a burger and fries as you drive down the interstate, or driving when sleepy and struggling to keeps your eyes open? Would you be a better driver if you developed good driving habits, such as, using your turn indicator before changing lanes, leaving a safe distance between you and the car ahead of you, and paying close attention as you drive down the highway?

What are steps to becoming a better driver? The first is to objectively identify what you do when you drive that is unwise. Often it is helpful to get honest feedback from someone who is with you when you drive. For instance, failing to check your blind spot in your side-view mirror before changing lanes may be a major issue that needs corrected. Once identified, you need to develop and then implement a plan to correct those unsafe driving habits.

Next, you need to identify those things you need to do more of to improve your driving. Making sure your car is maintained, driving at a safe speed, and applying Rain-X to your windshield to improve visibility in the rain are things one might do to be a better driver. Driving involves a variety of different skills.

In life, we need to do more of those things that are good for us and others, and less of those things that are bad for us or others in the same way we would work on being a better driver. Let's explore the topic of procrastination in more detail. Have you ever given much thought to why you procrastinate in the first place?

Why Do People Procrastinate?

One answer for why people procrastinate is negative reinforcement. Negative reinforcement is the strengthening of a behavior by the removal on an aversive experience. Let's imagine a young father taking his two-year-old daughter grocery shopping. As he places the groceries on the conveyor belt at the checkout, little Lily eyes a candy bar. Dad says no to

Lily's demand for the candy bar. Lily throws a major temper tantrum with screaming, tears, and snot flowing down her lip. His anxiety spikes as he senses everyone staring at him. In his emotional state of mind, he believes others think he is abusing his little girl. He buys the candy bar for her, and her screaming and tears immediately stop. ***The negative reinforcement of reduced anxiety will make it more likely that Lilly's dad will give into her demands the next time she throws a temper tantrum in public.***

In the above scenario, Lily's temper tantrum is strengthened through positive reinforcement. ***Getting the candy bar will strengthen Lily's behavior of screaming and crying.*** Positive reinforcement is the strengthening of a behavior by following it with a pleasant or desired event. It is interesting to note that often negative reinforcement, removal of an unpleasant experience, is more powerful than positive reinforcement. Immediate consequences in the form of negative or positive reinforcement are powerful rewards that can lead to habits. And procrastination is an ineffective habit.

How Does One Overcome Procrastination?

As I am writing this book, I am aware that there are times when focusing on writing is difficult. If I give into the temptation to play computer games, then I will experience both negative and positive reinforcement. The negative reinforcement would be the immediate removal of the anxiety and discomfort of trying to articulate ideas in writing. The positive reinforcement would be doing something fun, such as, winning the next video game. If I do give into my urge, then over time I will be playing more and more computer games and writing much less. So how can I win out over the strength of negative and positive reinforcement?

I am aware of a number of my human weaknesses and of having a choice. I have set a rule for myself. The rule is no playing computer games when I'm doing my writing. I set a timer for 30 minutes and stick to the task of writing, until the timer goes off. If I feel I am finished writing for a while after the timer goes off, then I can go for a walk outside, get a drink of water, or play a computer game. In simple terms I finish my work before I play. And my play becomes a positive reinforcement for completing my work.

There are things I do that help me to keep my mind focused on the goal. I have affirmations I read during my morning routine, that remind me of why I write and what I hope to accomplish. I feel good when I see my book progressing. I am hopeful that the book will help readers become psychologically strong. I also visualize my book being completed and in print. I even imagine feeling proud and happy to have written a self-help book that outlines steps for experiencing a more meaningful and happier life.

The Benefits of Having a Morning Routine

Please pay close attention to the idea of developing a morning routine to start your day off in a positive manner. I believe this idea could prove to have a huge impact on your life. I believe developing a positive morning routine is a secret to psychological strength.

I've had a morning routine for many years, but I recently read a book that has improved my routine. The book is, *The Miracle Morning,* by Hal Elrod. Hal writes about reading a number of autobiographies of famous people and finding key activities that they have in common. He found that many successful people start out with one or more activities he refers to as Life SAVERS. SAVERS is an acronym for:

S Silence (Meditation and prayer)
A Affirmations
V Visualization
E Exercise
R Reading
S Scribing (Writing or journaling)

I strongly encourage you to develop a morning routine, even if it is only 15 to 30 minutes in length. My morning routine starts out with turning my alarm off, getting out of bed and going to the restroom, dressing in my workout clothes, and drinking a glass of water to hydrate my body. I then read for 5 to 10 minutes, and do my morning meditation and pray. Next, I read my affirmations I've written for being a better person and a better writer. I then turn to my "future journal" where I write about what I hope happens as if it had already been accomplished. On a particular day, I will write about feeling grateful and good about helping my clients, eating healthy, writing creatively, and spending time with family and friends in a positive activity. I also close my eyes and visualize doing these things and enjoying it. I then do a workout routine with exercise equipment.

My morning routine usually takes 30 to 75 minutes. It starts my day off in a positive manner, and I find it to be both enjoyable and energizing. On several mornings I play racquetball, and do the other parts of my routine after I come home and shower. Exercise is quite important for one's physical and mental health. It helps free our bodies of stress, and it gives us energy. Doing my morning routine helps me to be more productive, and it contributes to me being a happier and healthier person.

Setting Effective Goals

I believe having some meaningful goals gives my life focus and helps me to find happiness. As I write this I am looking forward to teaching a six-week mindful parenting class. I have taught this particular class three previous times, and I always enjoy challenging parents to explore new ways to strengthen their relationship with their kids. I have taught a number of parenting classes during my life, and I have written a book titled, *How to Parent Mindfully with Emotional Control, Love and Strength.*

Finding that middle path between being overly goal driven and being unmotivated and aimless is important. Do you have some meaningful goals that are important to you? Do you make time to enjoy life and experience peace of mind? Are your goals something more than accumulating money and possessions? Does achieving your goals benefit others as well as yourself?

How Is an Effective Goal Written?

It is important to write your goals out. Most people find that they are more likely to achieve goals when they are written down, instead of just thinking about them. When you write your daily goals, make sure you observe the four requirements of writing an effective goal. The requirements are: a goal needs to be observable, measurable, doable, and have a timeline.

If I write that ***my goal is to be happy***, then I have failed to meet the four requirements of writing a good goal. Happy is not observable. Smiling is observable, and so is laughing. There is no measurement of being happy as the goal is written above. Smiling at least three times is measurable. Smiling is also doable. You are obviously capable of smiling. Finally, there is not a specific timeline for the "be happy" goal. Persons are more motivated to achieve a goal when it meets the requirements of being an effective goal.

If you want to become healthy by exercising, which of the following goals meet the requirement of being observable, measurable, doable, with a specific timeline?

Goal 1: I will work out before lunch.

Goal 2: I will walk outside for 30 minutes before 6:00 PM today.

Goal 3: I will run a 5K (3.1 miles) in 11 minutes today.

Goal 2 is the only one that meets the four requirements. Goal 1 is not measurable and working out is vague. Does working out mean lifting weights, running on a treadmill, or repeatedly lifting a hotdog to your mouth until it's consumed? Goal 3 is not doable, because even the best athlete is unable to run 3.1 miles in 11 minutes.

Long Term vs. Short Term Goals

It is helpful to have both long-term and short-term goals. I have a long- term goal of weighing 178 pounds or less by December 31st. of this year. That means I need to lose 10 pounds in the next two months. My short-term goal for today was to eat only at mealtime, to not eat bread or refined sugar, and to exercise by playing three games of racquetball. By setting daily goals like the above, I am more likely to reach my long-term goal.

Persons often fail to meet goals because they set too many of them, do not have the time needed to achieve them, and are not truly committed to doing what it takes. I could start writing on five or even ten books. Doing that would greatly sabotage the chances of getting any of them completed. It is wise to focus on just a few goals, and to be 100% committed to working on those goals.

It is helpful to me to clarify the reason for setting and working on a specific goal. I am wanting to lose weight for the following reasons. My mother died at age 85 from Alzheimer's and other health issues. In my reading I have discovered that there are a number of things that a person can do to improve their brain health, and to possibly prevent or delay the onset of Alzheimer's.

The following are reasons why I would like to lose weight. Regular exercise and losing excess weight have both been cited as important in maintaining a healthy brain. Proper diet with a lot of fresh vegetables and fruits is another factor in maintaining brain health. I want to lessen the strain on joints, especially my knees to allow me to continue to play racquetball and go hiking. Having important health reasons for losing weight motivates me to be serious about eating wisely and doing regular exercise.

If you were to set just one or two long-range goals, what would they be? Would they relate to physical health, mental health, spiritual growth, recreation, improved relationships, or doing something you feel would contribute to bettering others? What short-term goal might you write today?

Why Do We Need to Develop Positive Habits?

Good habits can radically improve our lives, and bad habits can over time destroy us. A habit becomes something we do automatically without having to exert a great deal of thought or effort. Good habits allow us to use our willpower wisely. Each day we wake up with a finite amount of willpower, and each time we have to think hard or say no to a temptation we use up some of that willpower. It is when our willpower battery is nearly depleted that we do those things we don't want to do, and fail to do those things we are committed to do.

How Do We Deplete Our Willpower?

Samantha wakes after a restful sleep when her alarm goes off and her willpower battery is charged at 100%, like your cell phone is once it is fully charged. She has made a commitment to go for a 20-minute run and she's not a runner. At the end of her morning run her willpower charge has dropped to 75%. She has to struggle with the kids to get them up and ready for school. She uses her willpower to be patient and skillful in getting them ready. Now her battery charge is at 60%. She is dieting and avoiding sweets, and finds her husband has cooked blueberry pancakes with warmed maple syrup. She again uses her willpower and eats an apple and yogurt, and now her willpower charge is at 50% and she hasn't even left the house.

During the day, Dawn has to make important decisions at work, and by the time she gets home her willpower charge is at 15%. After cooking dinner and getting her kids to bed her willpower is at 5%. She's tired and hungry and her willpower is practically depleted. Dawn eats a bowl of ice cream, and follows it with a second with hot fudge and whipped cream. Her husband comes in and sees her pigging out after not eating pancakes in the morning, and pokes fun at her. With depleted willpower she snaps at him and calls him a jerk, and leaves the kitchen with self-critical thoughts and feelings of anger and shame.

How Do We Charge Our Willpower Battery?

Willpower is considered key for living a successful life by some social psychologists. We need to learn to use our willpower wisely so we don't quickly exhaust it. Forming good habits and breaking bad habits is essential to living a more productive life. Let's look at several ways we can recharge our willpower during the day.

Eating healthy foods is quite important in building our willpower. Low glucose is correlated with decreased willpower. Although drinking a pop or eating a candy bar can rapidly give us increased glucose and willpower, the positive effects quickly wear off and we will experience a sugar crash. The person who eats healthy foods with adequate protein will sustain a healthy glucose level over a much longer period of time. Skipping lunch to get more work done may not be a wise thing to do.

Reducing stress by taking a break, taking slow deep breaths, or doing a pleasant exercise can help recharge our willpower battery. Talking with supportive persons is a good stress reducer. Often a change of scenery can help as well. Identifying a negative and irrational thought, and replacing it with a more positive thought can also reduce the energy drain on our willpower.

Reducing struggles with temptations is certainly helpful in maintaining a charged battery. If we use willpower when we shop to not buy junk food, then we can prevent the energy drain of not eating ice cream when we open the freezer door at night. If there are no cookies in the house, we don't have to waste our willpower on saying no to the double cream Oreos repeatedly throughout the day. It is wise to be proactive in our battle against bad habits, instead of putting ourselves into highly tempting situations.

Next, we will need to look at what we can do to develop good habits, and to conquer our bad habits. Habits are formed through repetition and practice. ***Developing good habits is vital to becoming psychologically strong***.

The Twenty-Second Rule

Shawn Achor, author of *The Happiness Advantage, writes about the power of the* ***Twenty-***

Second Rule. He learned that persons often continue to do something of little value over something that would be of greater value to them, because it requires more willpower to change that which is a habit. He shows how he effectively utilized the twenty-second rule to overcome his problem.

Shawn Achor wanted to play his guitar, but when he arrived home he found that it was easier to turn the TV remote on and watch television than play his guitar. Trying to do it by willpower alone, Shawn miserably failed. Then he thought of a simple solution that proved to be successful.

Shawn decided that he would buy a guitar stand so he would see it when her first entered his living area, and not have to go to the closet and remove it from the case. He made the activity he wanted to do a little easier and twenty seconds faster to do. Then he took the batteries out of the remote and placed them in a bedroom drawer. He simply made TV watching a little harder and twenty seconds longer to do. These two simple steps proved effective in helping him watch much less TV and play his guitar more.

Five Steps for Developing Healthy Habits

STEP 1: Start with only one good habit you want to do more and one unhealthy habit you want to do less. Stan wants to do better in his evening college course. He often has depleted willpower in the evening, and after opening his course book to study he feels fatigued and unmotivated. He says to himself, I'll study later and turns on the TV. Soon he has watched several mindless programs and has spent an equal amount of time channel surfing. For Stan, step one might be to spend more time focused on studying and cutting out TV watching on those nights when he needs to study. It is most important that Stan focus on just those two goals, or he will deplete his willpower on other things and accomplish none of them.

STEP 2: Develop a realistic plan as to how to increase action on the positive habit and to spend less time doing the negative habit. Stan plans to study in 30-minute intervals and will use the timer on his phone as a reminder. After completing a study period, he allows himself a five-minute break in which he will walk away from the desk and get a non-alcoholic beverage. He makes a rule that on study nights he will not watch TV until his studies have been completed or he has studied for at least 90 minutes.

Step 3: Set a realistic goal that is both challenging and doable. Stan believes setting the goal *of "studying until his homework is completed or studying for 90 minutes for at least 12 of the next 30 days*" is both doable and a challenge. He guesses that he only reached that goal around 4 or 5 times in the past 30 days. He also sets a goal of *watching no TV in the evening for 8 days in a row over the next 30 days.*

STEP 4: Chart or track progress on doing more of the positive habit and less of the negative habit.

Stan made a simple chart on his computer and printed a hard copy. He started tracking how many days in a row he studies for at least 90 minutes or until his homework is completed. He also tracked how many days in a row he watches no TV or does not turn the TV on until his homework is completed. It is easier to break a positive behavior pattern when we have done it for only two or three days, then when we have done it for 30 days in a row.

STEP 5: Find an accountability partner to hold you accountable for working on and achieving your goal. Stan told Amy, a good friend, about his plan to increase his study time and decrease his TV watching. He agreed to check in with her every Thursday evening to report his progress. At the end of the month, Stan had reached his goal and met his study objective 17 times. At one point he had met his study objective for 7 straight days. Amy told Stan she was proud of his effort. She pointed out that he had significantly improved his study habits and was wasting less time on TV.

I would like to share with you the conquering procrastination worksheet I use in my practice. There is room for seven days on the actual worksheet, instead of the four you see on the next page. Wins are successes you have with your goal, and losses are setbacks. Your correction plan is what you need to change next to achieve your goal.

CONQUERING PROCRASTINATION WORKSHEET

Specific Goal:

____

Day/Date: ______ **Wins:** ______________________

____

Losses: ______________________________________

Correction Plan: ______________________________

____

Day/Date: ______ **Wins:** ______________________

____

Losses: ______________________________________

Correction Plan: ______________________________

____

Day/Date: ______ **Wins:** ______________________

____

Losses: ______________________________________

Correction Plan: ______________________________

____

Day/Date: ______ **Wins:** ______________________

____

Losses: ______________________________________

Correction Plan: ______________________________

____

Now is your chance to build healthy habits and conquer procrastination. Focus on doing one or more of the following activities to become psychologically strong.

Activities to Build Psychological Strength

1. **Just be aware of your procrastination and its consequences.** Notice the times you avoid doing something that is difficult and unpleasant, and identify what you do instead to comfort yourself or reduce your stress. Understand that almost everyone procrastinates, and set your mind to procrastinate less to be more effective.

2. **Start a morning routine.** Plan to get up 30 to 60 minutes earlier and develop your personal morning routine. Consider doing 10 minutes of exercise, some motivational reading, prayer or meditation, and visualization of reaching your goals.

3. **Use your willpower wisely.** Remember that you have a limited supply of willpower and you can easily exhaust it. Make sure your willpower battery is fully charged by getting adequate sleep, eating nutritious foods, and avoiding ruminating thoughts. Plan ways to avoid being in tempting situations when possible.

4. **Write effective goals.** Remember that an effective goal is observable, measurable, doable, and has a timeline.

5. Visualize daily personal goals you want to achieve. For example, if you want to run a marathon it would be important for you to do the following. Identify the reason for running the marathon (improve health and belief in yourself). Visualize successfully training, then running it, and crossing the finish line. In your mind feel tremendous pride for your accomplishment.

6. Identify several activities of importance that you want to do more and several things you want to do less. After you identify a number of activities to increase and a number to decrease, focus on just one to do more and one to do less. By narrowing your focus, you greatly increase your chances of building one good habit and decreasing one negative one.

7. Review and use the five steps for developing healthy habits. Refer to the five steps often as you work on developing healthy habits that can make your life more productive. Don't forget to be accountable to yourself, and realize the benefit of having an accountability partner.

Chapter 6: Relationship Empowerment
Becoming a Better Driver

SECRET: Others cannot make you feel bad unless you surrender your power to them by buying into negative beliefs, and you can develop skills to strengthen and maintain positive relationships by being more validating and showing compassion.

I am excited to share ideas from this chapter with you, because I want you to learn that others cannot make you feel bad without your permission. Yes, I understand that words can hurt more than physical pain. Yes, I understand that many persons have been damaged by what sick people have said to them. It is not what others say that hurts you, but it is what you believe about their words that actually affects you. You can become mentally and emotionally strong so that what others say and do will become less hurtful to you.

You also will be shown the benefits of stopping your efforts to control others. Our efforts to try to change others leads to increased anxiety, frustration, anger, and defensive outbursts. I will show you how conflict resolution skills can help you to get what you want without violating the rights of others.

We will revisit the protective child mindset that was introduced in chapter two. Failure to recognize the protective child in oneself and others leads to conflict. Awareness and understanding how it works can assist us greatly in our relationships with others. I hope that this chapter will give you skills to improve your relationships with others.

Becoming a Better Driver

When you're driving in busy traffic, you often need to go with the flow of traffic. You are more likely to have problems if you drive too fast or too slow. Better drivers communicate their intentions by using their turn indicators before changing lanes. They also avoid tailgating the car in front of them. They are respectful of others drivers. If you want to be more effective in navigating interactions with others, then I suggest you read on and adapt many of the skills suggested in this chapter.

What Is Relationship Empowerment?

Relationship empowerment is defined as the skill of taking ownership of your thoughts and feelings in interacting with others, and of no longer allowing others to control you through guilt trips, intimidation, criticism, or other persuasive strategies. Life becomes more manageable when you recognize that you cannot control others, and that others have no more control over you than what you give them. Much of our suffering in relationships comes directly from our thoughts and not from the actions of others.

The Story of Sidney and Power Surrender

Sidney has been in an abusive marriage for the past three years. Her husband is an alcoholic and frequently says hurtful and abusive things. At times he becomes irrationally jealous, and has on several occasions struck her in the face with his fist.

Sidney feels trapped and believes she has to stay in the marriage. At times she wants to leave her husband, but doesn't do so because of a number of beliefs she has. She has come to believe she is stupid and incapable, in part, because he told her she was on numerous times. She believes she would be a complete failure, if she were to divorce him. She is easily influenced by both his intimidation and his guilt trips. She also believes he needs her and would be incapable of taking care of himself should she leave.

Sidney doesn't realize it, but she has become a victim of her own "power surrender." Power surrender is when we allow others to control us by giving them control over us. She has surrendered her power to her husband. She has over time lost confidence in herself, and on a daily basis allows her husband to influence her beliefs. She tends to repeatedly tell herself that she is trapped and there is nothing she can do about it. Her negative beliefs trigger feelings of helplessness and hopelessness. The more she practices this power surrender, the harder it becomes for her to take control of her life.

It is important to understand that others have the capability of physically harming us. Sidney certainly could be injured or even killed by her husband should he discover that she has plans to leave him. It is also true that she could be injured or even killed should she remain in the abusive relationship. But he can only mentally harm her to the extent that she embraces the beliefs that he encourages through his critical remarks, guilt trips, intimidation, and other persuasive strategies.

Developing Relationship Empowerment

There are a number of skills Sidney could develop to experience relationship empowerment. The first skill is called ***reality acceptance.*** It is the ability to see and accept things as they really are. Sidney would certainly benefit from understanding that her husband is both an alcoholic and an abusive spouse. She would also profit from understanding that she has over time developed a number of irrational beliefs that continue to keep her stuck in a very unhealthy relationship.

Frequently individuals choose to see others the way they want them to be or the way they think they should be. This leads to repeated frustration and discouragement. Ask yourself these two questions. Do I have any factual reason to expect this person to act differently? Am I setting myself up to be disappointed and discouraged by expecting this person to act differently?

A second skill that could prove helpful to Sidney is ***validation power.*** This is the skill of saying validating things to persons who verbally attempt to control us without buying into what they say. How could Sidney use validation power to respond to her husband saying, *"You're a stupid idiot. You can't even fix scrambled eggs without burning them."* She could respond, *"You have every right to be angry, because the eggs are burned."* If she calmly says this without buying into the accusation that she is a stupid idiot, then maybe he will calm down. It is often difficult for persons to continue to attack us when we don't argue with them or defend ourselves.

If later in the day Sidney's mother calls, how could Sidney use ***validation power*** to respond to the remark, *"I can't believe that you stay with a man who* *treats you like that."* She could say something like, *"Mom, you have a good point. I'm not sure why I've stayed with him as long as I have."* As Sidney learns to use validation power, she may be surprised to discover she is taking more control over her feelings, and not allowing others to influence her as much as she has in the past.

A third skill is ***limit setting.*** It can be said that we teach others how to treat us. If we allow others to call us names, then in a way we are unintentionally teaching them to be disrespectful to us. Limit setting involves telling others NO when we don't want to do something. It may also involve telling others we will not put up with their actions, and if the actions continue what we will do about it. Sidney could tell her husband, when he is calm and sober, that she will not tolerate being beaten by him again, and should he do it she will call the police and divorce him.

Certainly, one needs to be prepared to deal with the probable response of another, and if her husband is unusually violent it may be wiser for her to go to a woman's shelter and take legal action from there. Sidney could also learn to tell her husband "no" when he asks her to call his boss and tell him he's sick when he's hung over from drinking. The longer we have given into others, the more difficult it is to do things differently because a pattern of unhealthy expectations has been established. No matter how long we have done something, it is possible to change.

Be Aware of the Protective Child Mindset

In chapter two, the ***protective child mindset*** was defined as "***an ineffective way of perceiving and reacting to the world with the goal of feeling important and gaining recognition."*** Most of us carry around memories of bad feelings associated with thoughts of "not being good enough" from childhood. When those memories are triggered, the present reality becomes distorted and those "not okay feelings" often lead us to think and react in a protective and almost childlike manner.

Becoming aware that both ourselves and others often enter this protective child mindset is vital to improving our relationships. If we recognize that we are becoming defensive (a sure sign that we entered the protective child mindset), then we can take a couple slow, deep breaths and respond mindfully rather than react in an ineffective manner. Instead of judging ourselves, it is helpful to show curiosity about the things that trigger our defensiveness. It is helpful to be aware of how we think and feel when we're in the protective child state. Awareness gives us an opportunity to respond rather that react in fear or anger.

When we work at noticing our protective child mental state, we have taken a large step in controlling it. Without awareness it will control our lives, and create emotional pain and relationship problems. When we understand and accept that it exists, it loses much of its power to harm us. By showing compassion to ourselves and others, we can begin to respond to others with kindness and validation instead of attacking them. This type of response is more mature and effective.

When we truly recognize our protective child mindset, then we can see that others too have their own protective child. It is not our job to point this out to them, but we can convey empathy and treat them in a more compassionate manner. We can work on developing a more understanding and forgiving heart.

The Story of Jan and David

Jan and David had been married for a couple years, and they were having frequent fights. David would come home and see the dirty dishes stacked on the kitchen counter and dirty pans on the stove. He would immediately think, "What the hell did Jan do all day? I worked hard busting my ass and she just lays around watching TV." He'd walk into the living room and glare at his wife as she watched TV. Then he'd shout, *"Jan you haven't done anything around the house, have you?"*

Jan would immediately become tearful, stomp to the bedroom and slam the door locking it behind her. She would think to herself, *"I hate him. My life has been miserable this past year. All he does is bitch and gripe at me. If he treated me with some decency, I'd have the energy to do some housework."* She would stay in the bedroom until her hunger prompted her to go to the kitchen and eat some junk food to calm her emotional pain.

It is easy to recognize that both David and Jan were thinking and reacting from their protective child mindset. You can imagine how each would feel, and how ineffective their actions were in attempting to improve their relationship and to feel good. Over time the couple was drifting further and further apart. Then Jan spoke to a good friend who taught her about the protective child mindset. She was cautioned to not blame David, but instead to try to first work on recognizing and correcting her unhealthy pattern of thinking, feeling, and acting.

The next day when David got home, Jan had the kitchen dishes and pots and pans cleaned. She knew that David might still complain about anything that bothered him, and she accepted she had no control over what he said and did. She greeted him and asked him how his day had gone. He responded, "Same old, same old." She then told him she appreciated him working hard and making it possible for them having a nice house to live in. Her kind words and efforts to tidy the house started the evening off on a better foot.

Later, David snapped at her for putting onions in the green beans. Jan did not tear up, and she did not run and hide in the bedroom. Instead she said calmly, *"Sorry, I forgot you don't like onions in your beans. I'll try to remember that the next time I fix them. I would appreciate it if you would tell me calmly and not raise your voice. Does that sound reasonable to you?"* This awareness of her protective child state of mind became helpful to Jan. She realized that in time she could explain to David what she had learned from her friend. She now needed to focus on changing herself. She would have plenty of time to figure out how she could respond differently to David, and what she would need to do to stand up for herself.

Effective Listening

Listening is an important part of all communication. Some people listen deeply, some listen superficially, and some hardly listen at all. If you want to have a close and intimate relationship with another person, you will need to listen deeply at times. When a person listens deeply, he or she is keenly focused on trying to understand how the other person is thinking and feeling in that moment. They listen without judging, and they convey an awareness of why the person thinks and feels the way they do. They get the other person.

Being an effective listener involves a whole array of skills. Direct eye contact, paying attention, open body language, and asking questions to show interest are important. In addition, a good listener will reflect what the other person is feeling in words that are tentative. If Mary's voice shows signs of hostility toward John forgetting her birthday, a good listener would <u>not</u> say, *"I know exactly how you feel."* Instead an effective listener would say something like, *"It sounds like you are really angry at John, and what he did must have hurt your feelings."* This allows Mary to say yes or no and to clarify if she has been understood.

Strive to be a good listener. Realize there are times when your total and undivided attention is wanted and needed. There are going to be other times when more casual listening is perfectly okay. If you practice showing genuine interest and being non-judgmental, you will improve your listening skills and those you care about will appreciate your attentive listening.

Assertive Communication

Communication styles are often broken down into aggressive, passive, and assertive. We will discuss each one of these communication styles, and you need to know that there are certain times when each of them is appropriate. However, only one of the styles proves to be effective in most situations.

When people communicate aggressively they stand up for their rights, but they do it in a way that violates the rights of others. Persons who are frequently aggressive are likely to experience more conflict. They may lose friends and relationships, because people do not like to have their feelings trampled on or be controlled by a bully. Persons are more likely to lose a job, get in a fight, or get in trouble when they are aggressive. Loneliness is often the consequence of being overly aggressive with others.

People who are passive fail to stand up for themselves or to speak up for their rights. Passive individuals are more likely to be taken advantage of by others. They often feel angry and resentful. Over time their self-esteem falls and they lose confidence in themselves. Passive persons are more likely to experience depression, because they turn their anger inward. They tend to lose respect of others, and are likely to have difficulty in their relationships.

Persons who communicate assertively, stand up for themselves when appropriate to do so. They do it in a way that respects the rights of others. They respond mindfully, instead of reacting impulsively. They act wisely, instead of reacting from the protective child. They are more likely to be listened to, because they act in a way that is less likely to trigger defensiveness. Persons who communicate assertively appear more confident that than those who are passive or aggressive.

With what I have explained, why would it ever be advantageous to act in a passive or an aggressive manner? If a man walked up to you in a parking lot and he pointed a gun at you demanding your money, what would you do? If you value your life, you're probably going to be passive and hand your money to the person holding the gun. On the other hand, if a person attacked you in your home and started choking you, you're probably going to fight back for your life. Aggressiveness, in that situation, may be the only action that would save your life. However, in most situations assertiveness is a wiser and more effective way of responding.

Pay close attention to the conflict resolution model to be explained next. It is most useful in dealing with conflict.

Conflict Resolution Model

The following are steps you can use to communicate in as assertive manner when you experience conflict with another. Marsha Linehan refers to these four steps as the DEAR MAN skill in her *DBT Skills Manual.* Here are the four steps:

1. **Describe the situation in an objective manner without blame.** Example: *When you called me at work this morning and told me to pick up milk and bread from the grocery store without asking if it was a good time to talk was a problem for me.*

2. **Express your feelings and thoughts about the situation in an objective manner.** Example: *I felt embarrassed and annoyed, because I was talking with a co-worker about our project. I thought it would have been nice if you had first asked if I could talk before telling me what you wanted me to do for you.*

3. **State your request in a direct and honest manner.** Example: *When you call me at work, I would like you to check and see if it is convenient for me to talk before getting into a conversation. There will be times I will need to call you back, if I'm in the middle of something.*

4. **Strengthen the request by giving a reason why it is beneficial to the other person or the relationship.** Example: *If you will do this, I would appreciate it and feel like you are respecting me at work, and I won't be annoyed with you.*

I encourage you to learn to use these four simple steps. I took an assertive communication class in college many years ago, in which the first three steps were taught. I am most grateful for them, and feel they've had a positive impact on my life.

Conflict Resolution with Jan and David

Let's revisit the story of Jan and David discussed earlier in the chapter. David could have used conflict resolution when he arrived home and found the kitchen trashed and his wife watching TV. It would have played out something like this.

David took a few slow, deep breaths to calm himself when he saw the dirty dishes on the counter and the dirty pans on the range. He gave Jan the benefit of doubt by being nonjudgmental. He considered she may not be feeling well, or that she might be depressed.

David then entered the living room and started the conflict resolution communication. He said calmly, "Jan, I would like to talk to you and ask your help in figuring out a problem I have. When would be a good time for us to talk?"

Jan said, "Now's fine."

David said, "Is it okay if I turn the TV off, so it doesn't distract us?"

Jan said, "Sure."

David broke the ice by saying, "I love you and I want us to solve our differences by talking them out and not blaming each other."

David then launched into the four steps of the conflict resolution plan. He said, "When I get home and find the dirty dishes and dirty pans on the counter and stove, I feel frustrated in part because I tend to be a neat freak. I also feel that if I work at a job to bring in money, that I'd like you to keep the house up. I would really appreciate you keeping the house tidier. If you work on this, I will try to help you more with taking turns cooking dinner. What do I need to do to support you more?"

Jan said, "I really want you to talk to me respectfully like you're doing now. When you get angry and yell at me, it hurts and then I don't feel like doing anything at home. If you help me do the dishes now, I'll cook us dinner."

David said, "You have a deal, I'll work on being less of a jerk. Let me change out of my work clothes and wash my hands, and I'll meet you in the kitchen in a few minutes to help you with the dishes."

Jan said, "I'd like that, and if you want I'll fix tacos when the dishes are done."

The two kissed and David headed to the bedroom to change out of his work clothes and to clean up.

Activities to Build Psychological Strength

1. Stop your power surrender. Understand that most of your suffering in relationships comes directly from your thoughts, and not from the actions of others. If you're in a destructive relationship, carefully plan how to get out of it. Stop allowing others to manipulate you by believing their critical words.

2. Be accepting of reality. Don't waste your time thinking that others should do what you want, or be the way you want them to be. When we see people as they are, we tend to stop being frustrated and angry.

3. Learn to validate others. Validation is a way of communicating that we understand how someone else feels through our words and actions. It helps us to connect with others, and when others are upset our validation can help them to calm down.

4. When needed, set and enforce reasonable limits. We have a responsibility to stand up for ourselves and to not allow others to walk over us. We need to respond mindfully by setting realistic limits, and enforcing them.

5. Develop effective listening skills. Others are unlikely to care much about what you have to say, if you fail to show you care about what they say. Show good eye contact, ask gentle questions, and reflect their thoughts and feelings back to them.

6. Learn to communicate assertively. Remember the disadvantages of being overly passive or overly aggressive. Communicate in a way that shows respect for both you and the other person.

7. Use the four-step conflict resolution plan. First state the situation or problem factually without placing blame. Describe how you feel and share your thoughts behind your feelings. State your request in a clear and specific way. Reinforce your assertion by stating how it would be helpful to the other person to meet your request.

Chapter 7: Responsibility Theft

Protecting Against Theft and Helping Others

SECRET: You harm yourself and those you intend to help when you deprive them of taking responsibility for their actions and from experiencing the consequences of their behavior.

I have no way of knowing if you struggle with saying "no" and doing too much to help others. If this is an area of concern for you, then you may want to pay special attention to this chapter. I have written it for parents who try too hard to protect their kids from the pain they must experience to grow. It is written for those who believe they are doing what is best for others, when those on the receiving end need to be doing much more for themselves. The five activities at the end of the chapter will help you find a healthy balance between giving and receiving.

A Driving Lesson to Protect Against Theft

Most persons have enough sense to not leave their car unlocked with the keys in it. Most would not be tempted to steal someone's car, if they found it unlocked with the keys. Unfortunately, those same people that would never think of stealing a car, often unintentionally rob those they care about of something far more precious than a vehicle. They unintentionally rob loved ones of the responsibility of learning to solve their own problems. The following story of Kristen illustrates this point.

The Story of Kristen

Kristin is a single parent of Liz, fourteen, and Jason, ten. For years she has worked very hard to provide for her two kids, and she has repeatedly sacrificed to give them things they wanted while she did without things she really needed. She is now wearing shoes that are falling apart, because she gave into Jason's pleas to get a pair of fashionable shoes that cost over $100.

Kristin also frequently defends her children's behavior at school when they are disrespectful to teachers or break rules. She explains that they don't have a father and Jason's attention deficit hyperactivity disorder makes it impossible for him to control his impulsive behavior. Kristin's mental strength is frequently low due to a lack of self-care, worry over the bills, and frustration over not being able to get her kids to do chores or school work. She finds herself frequently yelling at the kids, and reminds them of all the things she has sacrificed to make it possible for them to have the things they've wanted. Kristin is completely unaware that she has, for years, committed ***responsibility theft***.

Responsibility Theft Defined

Responsibility theft is taking action that deprives another of the opportunity to assume responsibility for one's own behavior and learn from the consequences of that behavior. Kristin has unintentionally taught her daughter and son over the years that they don't have to do their chores or school work. She has bailed them out, time and time again, by doing their responsibilities for them. This has deprived them of learning the consequences that most children experience when they don't perform their responsibilities.

A major cause of Kristin's behavior starts with the irrational belief that she's a bad mother, because she didn't marry the children's father. Because of this belief, she has felt guilty, even though the guilt is unjustified. She has worked way too hard trying to meet her kid's unrealistic demands. Unfortunately, her actions have robbed her children of the chance to develop responsibility. Instead they have acquired an attitude of entitlement. This attitude and irresponsible behavior repeatedly leads them into conflict with peers and persons in authority. Until they learn differently, Liz and Jason will continue to have frequent problems and experience negative feelings.

What Is Sacrifice Resentment?

Kristin experiences ***sacrifice resentment.*** She frequently feels resentful for all the sacrifices she has made for her children. She has worn herself out by working hard and trying to meet their demands. She and her children would be much better off, if she took better care of herself and made time to do things she enjoyed. Persons are less likely to feel resentment when they meet their own needs. Caretakers frequently wear out because they neglect their own physical and mental self-care, and they often feel resentful. Most do not hide their feelings of resentment well.

It is important to understand that responsibility theft can occur with children, parents, spouses, siblings, and practically anyone. Often the person has good intentions, but the consequences are often harmful for both the "responsibility thief" and the one denied the opportunity to learn responsibility.

Stopping Responsibility Theft

Persons who learned to be caring and giving, often are the ones most likely to develop responsibility theft. Unfortunately, they failed to learn when it is wise to give and when it is not. If you discover that you are a responsibility thief, please do not complicate things by self-blame and taking on more guilt. Instead, be aware of the negative consequences of responsibility theft, and work on changing this unhealthy pattern of behavior. Be prepared that others who have learned to lean on you, will resist your efforts to change. That is to be expected, and yet you need to change for their benefit as well as your own.

The following are suggested steps to breaking the habit of being a responsibility thief:

1. When you have the urge to rush in and help someone, first stop and ask yourself the following two questions. "Will my helping in the long run assist or harm the growth of the one I want to help?" "Am I helping because it is the right thing to do, or am I helping to avoid facing my own problems and responsibilities?"

2. Make it a practice when asked to help to say, "I need to think about this. I will get back with you later". Take as much time as needed to make a wise decision. Be aware of your protective child and desire to feel good by doing things to please others.

3. Say NO to helping in situations where you are likely to feel resentful if the person you plan to help fails to thank you or pay you back in some way. If you are apt to feel resentful, you probably are helping for the wrong reasons.

4. Say NO if you are likely to harm your physical or mental health in the process of helping. If you fail to adequately care for your physical and mental health, it would be wise to step back from committing to help.

Healthy Helping Vs. Unhealthy Helping

I do not want to discourage you from helping others, but I do want to warn you that helping others in the wrong way can be problematic for you and them. "Healthy helping" typically benefits both the person being helped and yourself. Unhealthy helping is doing something for others when it would be better for them to do it themselves.

If Jeff is severely injured in an auto accident, he may need hospital staff to push him in a wheelchair in the early stages of his recovery. As he heals and regains his ability to walk, Jeff must endure some pain and put forth effort. If a staff person continues to push Jeff around simply because that makes the staff person feel good, then Jeff is going to be delayed in his recovery.

A skilled nurse is going to encourage Jeff to do more and more as he is able. She may show a smile and provide words of encouragement as he takes his first painful steps after the accident. However, if Jeff tries to get her to do things for him that he can clearly do for himself, she will need to refuse the temptation to be helpful and say, "Jeff, you walked on your own to the toilet yesterday, and I am confident you can do it again."

What Are the Benefits of Helping Others?

Many people get so caught up in their ego, that they focus only on what benefits them. Love is extending ourselves to do what we believe is best for another. When we do that with no anticipation or expectation, we feel good. We may feel even better if our helping hand brings happiness to the other person, and he or she expresses gratitude for our help.

In life there are times when we benefit from giving, and there are other times when we benefit from receiving. A healthy person learns to value doing both, and they will enjoy helping others and feel appreciative when they receive help. The remainder of this chapter will highlight several different ways to help others in positive ways. It will also address the need to be a grateful recipient of help and acts of kindness.

Encouragement

Encouragement is a way of instilling courage in another person. It is slightly different than praise, and tends to be more helpful. Let's look at how Robert praises his son, and later encourages his son. See if you can understand why encouragement is more effective than praise.

When Brian, Robert's five-year-old son, picks up his toys, Robert says, "Good boy." Later when Brian colors a page, he again says, "Good boy." At dinnertime Brian finishes his meal, and looks up and smiles at his dad. At first, Dad says nothing and Brian tears up. Immediately Dad says, "Good job, son." Then Brian smiles.

After reading a mindful parenting book, Robert learns about the difference between praise and encouragement. He quickly realizes he has been using praise, and Brian is becoming dependent on it. That evening, Brian looks at books for over thirty minutes on his own. Robert walks into Brian's room and says, "Brian, I am really proud of how you have been reading books quietly in your room. Tell me a little about one of them you've been looking at." Brian quickly tells his dad about the book.

Later that day, Dad sees Brian helping his younger sister drink from her bottle. Robert says, "Thank you for helping Emily drink her juice. That was a kind thing to do." Brian looks up at Dad and smiles. Robert picks his son up and gives him a big hug and tells him he loves him.

Praise is something said that is a general statement that does not give specific information. "Good boy" does not give information as to what the person has done to receive the praise. There are times when children and even adults want frequent praise to ease their sense of not feeling good enough. It tends to be more of an extrinsic reward given by another.

On the other hand, praise is specific and gives the person receiving it information that can be internalized. "I am really proud of how you have been reading books quietly" tells Brian that reading books and playing quietly in his room is appreciated by his father. Over time Brian can feel proud himself when he is reading or able to play quietly in his room.

Most people feel good when they genuinely give encouragement to another person. Here are a few examples of encouraging statements:

"I realize it is difficult, and I have confidence you will pull through this. You are a good person and have inner strength I've see many times."

"You are a talented artist. I wish I could draw half as good as you do."

"You are so thoughtful. Your family is lucky to have you."

"There was a lot of wisdom in what you posted. It made me think, and I feel it may help a lot of people."

"You are such a kind and thoughtful friend."

Acts of Kindness

We can show kindness to others in many ways. Opening a door for someone, being a courteous driver, and taking a batch of cookies to new neighbor are a few examples. When going for a walk, some people will take a trash bag with them and pick up litter to make the walkway look nice for others.

There are people who enjoy paying for the food order of the person behind them in line. Getting a bunch of quarters and tossing them in a playground for children to find could be an act of kindness. Helping change a flat tire for someone in distress can feel good. There are countless ways of showing kindness, if you simply slow down and open your eyes.

Volunteer Work

I cannot think that there is a single person on the face of the earth who could not benefit in some way from the help of another. We are neither totally dependent on others or completely independent of others. You may see yourself as independent and not realize that you probably did not grow or raise all the food you eat, did not make the table and chairs that you use when eating, and did not make the glass from which you drink or the plate from which you eat. The reality is that we are all interdependent.

As I approach retirement age, I look forward to doing various types of volunteer work. I plan to look for volunteer work that is meaningful to me and that I believe will benefit others. I have no desire to do something that I hate, because there are so many things needed that I can enjoy doing.

I enjoy teaching mindful parenting classes, cooking meals in a food kitchen for the needy, and doing programs that will help others grow in a positive way. I would love to see mindfulness taught in more schools, and for people to understand the problems created when we criticize children and place undue stress on them. I feel genuinely happy and grateful when I'm able to lend help in a healthy way.

If you are not involved in doing some type of volunteer work now, then consider doing something that you will both enjoy and feel good about doing. Would you like to build houses for Habitat for Humanity? Would you like to volunteer in a church or hospital? Are you interested in the becoming a Big Brother or Big Sister? Would visiting the elderly and lonely in a nursing home be something you would enjoy? Would you like to volunteer to read to children in an elementary school? I encourage you to do something that will truly benefit others and yourself.

Activities to Build Psychological Strength

1. Don't deprive others of the opportunity to learn to solve their own problems. Be slow to give unsolicited advice or to help others when it would be better for them to do it themselves.

2. Ask yourself two questions before rushing in to help someone. The two questions are: "Will my helping in the long run assist or harm the growth of the one I want to help?" "Am I helping because it is the right thing to do, or am I helping to avoid facing my own problems and responsibilities?"

3. Become aware of when you feel resentment. Recognize that resentment can be an important clue that you need to do something differently. Avoid playing the martyr role. Remember that if you take care of yourself, you are less likely to feel resentful and you will be more pleasant to be around.

4. Be quick to offer encouragement to others. Many times, others would benefit more from our encouragement than from us doing their work for them. Show faith in others, and be careful not to underestimate their ability to do things.

5. Consider doing some type of meaningful volunteer work. Find work that is a match to your talents and interests. The best volunteer work is doing something you are passionate about and have the ability to do well. Often times we develop improved skill by doing something over and over.

Chapter 8: Developing Mindfulness

Driving with Eyes Focused and Fully Aware

SECRET: Learning to respond to difficulties in a mindful manner, and living life mindfully will bring more happiness and peace of mind.

I hope you enjoy this chapter and get a lot out of it. Responding mindfully is probably the most important skill to help a person grow in psychological strength. In the very first chapter, you learned that the STOP Skill helps us to turn off the fight-flight reaction and allows us to use a higher functioning part of our brain to make better decisions. The STOP Skill makes it possible for us to respond mindfully.

In this chapter you, will learn how automaticity and mindful responding are opposites. Both have value and it is important to learn how to take advantage of each. You will learn about the "what skills" and the "how skills" of mindfulness. You will also be encouraged to engage in practicing mindfulness, so that it will become a valuable part of your life.

Mindfulness is commonly explained as paying attention to the present moment without judging the situation or oneself. I often tell my clients that mindfulness is learning to control one's mind to avoid ruminating about past regrets and future worries. As you read this chapter, you will discover that mindfulness is a rather complex concept that involves a number of different skills.

Mindful Driving

There are times when you drive with your full attention, and other times when your mind is somewhere else. One time when I was driving home from work, I was worrying about a particular problem. I exited the interstate and had driven several blocks when I noticed momentarily that I had no idea where I was. Then, I realized I had taken the exit before the one I had intended. That is an example of driving in a robotic and mindless state of mind.

I suspect that there are countless accidents that are caused by mindless driving, and yet most drivers safely navigate roads and highways while thinking about something other than their driving at any given time. I can remember driving a scenic highway in Tennessee that I had never driven. I was very focused on my driving and on viewing the beautiful landscape surrounding the highway.

In living our lives, we can be so caught up with the busyness of the day that we are completely unaware of the beauty of the life that is right in front of our eyes. I often encourage clients to take walks outside and to focus on nature. I remember one of my clients took a walk in a beautiful park following a heated argument with his son. He told me that he had not seen any of the beauty of the park, because he was recounting the argument between he and his son the entire time he walked. If we're not careful we will miss much of the beauty in our life by allowing our mind to wander from the present moment. Developing mindfulness prevents us from doing that.

Automaticity and Mindfulness

In chapter four, you learned that dialectical thinking allows one to hold two opposing beliefs as being true at the same time. Automaticity is good because it frees us of having to expend mental strength by doing things out of habit. Mindfulness is good because it helps us to focus on the present moment, to let go of distracting thoughts, and to make wise decisions. Although mindfulness and automaticity are opposites, both serve important functions.

I want to encourage you to form healthy habits that will guide you to do things automatically, and I also want you to learn to devote more time to responding in a thoughtful and mindful way. We will look at how these two opposing strategies could help someone lose weight and develop successful writing habits.

Effective Weight Loss

If you want a sustainable weight loss lifestyle, I would encourage you to read Susan Peirce Thompson's book titled, *Bright Line Eating: The Science of Living Happy, Thin, and Free.* Dr. Thompson is an Adjunct Associate Professor of Brain and Cognitive Sciences at the University of Rochester, an expert in the psychology of eating, and a successful recovering food addict. In her book, she strongly encourages you to read and understand the science behind why typical weight loss plans are ineffective.

After sharing research on food addiction and her personal battle in managing her addiction, she discusses the four bright lines of effective weight loss she uses. One of the chapters in her book is titled, "Automaticity: Your New Best Friend." Dr. Thompson explains that without developing effective habits of eating, one will succumb to the willpower gap. Each of us is hardwired to eat as a survival skill when our primitive mind tells us to do so. When our willpower is low, we will fall back on old and ineffective patterns of eating.

I believe that effective and sustainable weight loss involves learning what is essential to know, and then developing automatic and effective eating habits. I think it is also interesting to read that Dr. Thompson discourages exercise during the initial weight loss process for most people, because they need to save their willpower to focus on eating correctly. After they reach their goal weight and maintain it, she then encourages them to exercise to reap the many benefits it provides.

Mindfulness and Automaticity in Writing

As I write this book, I'm aware that I'm using both mindfulness and automaticity. When I do something automatically and habitually, I no longer have to exert enormous willpower. At this time, I have gone 38 days in a row of writing for at least 30 minutes each day. I am committed to writing 30 minutes a day unless I am traveling. By doing this I am developing the positive habit of writing every day. This helps me to get more writing in, and to avoid the bad habit of skipping it on a particular day. I now set a timer for 30 minutes when I start writing, and I don't stop until the timer goes off. If I feel like writing more, I will set the timer for 30 more minutes.

While I am writing, I strive to be focused and mindful as I explain the various concepts in this book. Later, I will go back and edit what I have written. Still later I will have someone else read parts of my manuscript, and will ask them to give me helpful feedback. It is quite clear to me that I need to develop positive habits of writing, and at the same time I need to focus my mind on what I am writing in that moment.

Essential Aspects of Mindfulness

Earlier in this chapter, I mentioned that mindfulness is a complex concept that involves a number of different skills. As a therapist doing dialectical behavior therapy (DBT), I've taught the how and what skills of mindfulness that were developed by Marcia Linehan. Dr. Linehan is a psychology professor, researcher, and therapist who developed DBT.

There are three what skills and three how skills of mindfulness. I will briefly describe each of these six skills. I will also give examples of how to use these skills, and inform you about some of the advantages of doing so.

The Three What Skills

Observe is the first what skill of mindfulness. It is one of three things that a person can do to be mindful. When we use the observe skill, we simply ***just notice*** what we are experiencing. As you walk you could might hear the sound of your shoes hitting the sidewalk, feel the warmth of sunshine on your face, hear the noise of a bird singing, or feel the sensation of your leg muscles as you walk. Often the first step of changing our emotional response is to first notice the specific emotion we are feeling.

Describe is the second what skill. When we use the describe skill we ***put words on*** what we are experiencing. If we notice our physical response to hearing critical words from our boss is to have a pounding heart and clinching our fists, we might describe our emotion as being anger. Often, we have more control over our emotions when we accurately name them. It has been said that we need to "name it to tame it."

When using the describe skill, persons are able to differentiate the facts of a situation from the stories they make up in their head. If my boss tells me that I missed the deadline she gave me for completion of the project, the story I make up in my mind may be that she will fire me. If I accurately use the describe skill, I would think my boss told me I missed the deadline for the project and that is all I know at this time. By doing this we can prevent the needless suffering we create through catastrophic thinking.

The third what skill is the **participate** skill. When we participate we **completely throw ourselves into what we are doing**. To participate watching a major league baseball game means you might watch the game closely, cheer your favorite team on, and focus on what is going on right now in the game. We often enjoy things much more when we throw ourselves 100% into what we are doing. Being mindful usually requires us to be totally involved in what we are doing.

The Three How Skills

The three how skills of mindfulness are non-judgmentally, one mindfully, and effectively. These three skills can have a major impact on how we live our lives.

The first how skill is ***non-judgmentally.*** Being non-judgmental means that in our mind we **avoid labeling someone or something as good or bad**. There is a huge difference between thinking my cousin smokes marijuana versus thinking my cousin is a pothead and loser. When we use judgmental words like "pothead" and "loser" we usually intensify our own negative emotions. Our judgments bring us into conflict with others and creates inner conflict.

The primary benefit of learning to be non-judgmental is it that it helps us to experience more peace of mind. Road rage is caused by judgmental thoughts one driver has toward another. If the person were to think about the situation in a factual way, the anger experienced would be less and the impulse to do something hurtful would be eliminated. In so many different situations, we could lessen our intense emotions by simply taking a non-judgmental stance.

One-Mindfully means **doing one activity at a time with full awareness**. When we eat one-mindfully, we are fully focused on our sensations of eating. We are totally aware of the taste, texture, and coldness of the cherry-nut ice cream as we eat it. We are not watching TV or talking on the phone as we eat. We are just enjoying the experience of eating and savoring our cherry-nut ice cream. When we are walking one-mindfully, our focus is on what we experience as we walk. In that moment of walking we are not planning the evening meal or thinking about when we yelled at our child earlier in the morning.

The third how skill is ***effectively***. In simple terms, doing something effectively means **doing what works**. If we are in a traffic jam and know a better way to get to our destination, effectively might mean we take the next exit to go a faster way. If our boss tells us to do something, it may mean doing it his or her way instead of arguing that our way is better. We may create problems for ourselves when we procrastinate mowing the lawn. Effectiveness may mean mowing the yard, instead of laying on the couch watching a TV program that has little value.

Practicing Mindfulness

There are numerous ways of practicing mindfulness. Formal mindfulness practice may involve some type of meditation. Sitting meditation is a common type of practice. It typically involves setting aside a specific amount of time to focus on one's breathing. As one sits erect and breaths in and out slowly, the mind will naturally wander. The person meditating simply recognizes the distracting thoughts, body sensations, sounds or other distractions and releases each and then returns the focus to breathing. In this respect, meditation is a way of training the mind to focus on one thing at a time.

Yoga and Tai Chi are standing meditations where one learns to focus on breathing and specific body movements. Both have health benefits, and also serve to train the mind to focus on one thing in the moment. There is much written and many videos available over the internet related to mindfulness meditations. Shortly, I will explain mindful walking exercises.

There are countless ways of practicing mindfulness informally. Whenever you focus your mind on doing one thing at a time in the present moment, you are practicing mindfulness. Mindful eating and doing other activities "one mindfully" will be discussed. I strongly encourage you to discover mindfulness practices that prove beneficial to you. Mindfulness can serve to relax your body, quiet your mind, and bring more happiness to your life.

Walking Mindfully

I will first explain the formal meditation practice of walking mindfully, and then I will discuss a simpler way of practicing mindful walking. The formal practice of walking mindfully is done slowly. A person places the heel of one foot forward, places it on the ground and lowers the toes to touch the ground. As the toes of the first foot touch the ground the heel of second foot is raised and then that foot is brought forward slowly as the heel is placed on the ground. This motion is repeated over and over. It is like walking in slow motion with one's mind focused on breathing and taking slow walking steps.

During the formal and slow walking meditation, some persons will take two or three steps on each inhale and two or three steps on each exhale. In one of the mindful walking audio CD's by Thich Nhat Han that I've listened to, he encourages an element of gratitude as one walks slowly. He will thank his feet for taking him where he wants to travel, and he will thank his heart for beating steadily and pumping life-giving blood throughout his body. He will thank his eyes for seeing beautiful things, and his ears for hearing the sound of birds singing as he walks.

An easier type of mindful walking can be done at a normal pace. When walking outside on a nice day, a person can be really focused on observing various sensory experiences. At times I will view a beautiful sunrise, smile at the budding trees, and treasure the warmth of the sunshine touching my face and arms. I will pay attention to the sound of my footsteps on the sidewalk, and look at the colorful spring flowers including daffodils and tulips. If I am having trouble focusing my mind, I may use the describe skill to use words to tell the story of what I see, hear, smell, and feel as I walk. There are times that I say to myself, "I experience the breeze on my face." "I experience the scent of honey suckle." "I experience the sound of a dog barking." "I experience the sensation of my arms and legs moving."

Mindful Eating

I often eat breakfast mindfully. It is the easiest meal for me to practice mindful eating, because I usually eat breakfast alone and there are fewer distractions. I will eat a bowl of cereal with banana slices and berries. When eating mindfully I take small bites and closely attend to the texture and taste of what I'm eating. I notice the noise made by chewing my cereal, and observe the sensation made when I swallow each bite. I notice the texture of the milk moistened shredded wheat, the softness and sweetness of the banana slices, and the tartness of the blueberries. I also experience thoughts of gratitude for the nutritious food I'm enjoying.

All you need to do to eat mindfully is to slow down and pay close attention to your sensory experiences as you eat your meal. Look closely at your food before you even take the first bite. Observe the aroma of the meal. Take slow bites and chew your food more that your normally do. Attend to the texture and flavor of what you're eating. Be aware of the gift you have to fuel your body, and enjoy the flavor of the nutritious food. Eating mindfully allows you to fully experience the present moment, and it is better for your health than stuffing your mouth and eating in a robotic manner.

One Mindfully

You can do almost any task mindfully by attending fully to the task at hand. You can wash your dishes mindfully, read a book mindfully, watch a TV program mindfully, fold your clothes mindfully, or talk to a family member or friend mindfully. As I mentioned earlier in this chapter, there are things that we can do automatically that allows us to focus our mind on other things while we are doing that task. That is okay and at times is desirable. But there are times when it is advantageous to do the task at hand with our full attention.

I would encourage you to practice mindfulness by paying complete attention to what you are doing at times during the day. Practice driving mindfully with your mind focused completely on the experience of driving your car. When your mind begins to wander, bring it back to the present moment and driving. In practicing this you are teaching your mind to attend to what you are doing in the now. If you succeed for only ten seconds, that is a step forward. Then you can strive to go for thirty seconds.

Learning to Respond Mindfully

The most important thing we need to learn is to respond mindfully to challenging situations, instead of reacting in an automatic and ineffective manner. If your child knocks over a glass of water, a momentary pause to think before reacting can have a powerful effect on both your life and the life of your child. A calm request to get a paper towel and wipe up the water can be much more effective than screaming, "Watch what you're doing!"

Our automatic reactions to situations often intensify both our emotions and the emotions of those around us. It is easy to develop the habit of reacting aggressively, and the more we act in anger the harder it is to respond mindfully. Fortunately, our minds are teachable. We first need to recognize how our thoughts intensify the feeling of anger and the urge to lash out. When we are able to calm down, it is important to plan more effective ways of responding when we become angry in the future.

Another Look at the STOP Skill

Do you remember the Stop Skill that was explained in chapter one? The STOP skill is important in learning to respond in a mindful manner. STOP is an acronym that outlines four important steps in responding mindfully instead of reacting impulsively. Here are the four steps:

1. **Stop before you make the situation worse.**
2. **Take slow, deep breaths and step back.**
3. **Open your mind to better options.**
4. **Proceed with respect and compassion.**

When we take the time to employ the above steps, we are incorporating mindful responding into our life. Just take a moment to reflect on how your life will improve when you start responding in a mindful way. Remember to use the STOP skill to begin the process of mindful responding.

The Story of Brandy and Her Mom

Before Brandy learned to respond mindfully, she had numerous arguments with her mother that often led to feelings of hurt and resentment. Mom would mention to Brandy that she needed to make more healthy food choices, and Brandy would immediately feel hurt and become defensive. Brandy would say things like: "If I wanted your opinion, I would have asked for it." "Don't talk about my eating, unless you want me to talk about your drinking." "I wouldn't eat so much, if you didn't continue to say things to make me feel like crap."

It is clear that the above responses Brandy made to her mother that they were both impulsive and ineffective. In therapy, Brandy discussed the adversarial relationship that had existed for years between she and her mother. Over time Brandy learned that she had a choice in not only what she said to her mother, but a choice in how she thinks and feels in response to what her mom said. At first it was hard for Brandy to grasp that her mother did not cause her feelings, but how she thought about what her mother said caused her feelings.

Brandy practiced with her therapist how to use the STOP skill, and how to respond to her mom in a non-defensive manner. Finally, she was prepared to speak with her mother in an effective manner. She went to visit her mom, and she was there only a few minutes when her mom said, "Brandy, I would like you to go to Weight Watchers, and I'm willing to help you pay for it." Brandy, excused herself and went to the bathroom. She took several slow, deep breaths and washed her face with cold water. She then thought about options, and was ready to reply non-defensively to her mom.

Brandy returned to the living room where she and her mom had been talking. She said, "Mom, I understand that you love me and would like me to lose weight. I appreciate the offer to help me pay for Weight Watchers. I may even take you up on your offer, but right now I am working with my therapist on losing weight. If you would like to help me, I would appreciate you simply asking how my weight loss plan is going. I am happy to tell you that I've lost six pounds in two weeks since starting my plan."

Brandy's mother said, "Brandy, Weight Watchers is a great program, and I believe they could help you more than your therapist."

Brandy calmly replied, "Weight Watchers is a long-standing weight loss program that has helped many people, but right now I'm going to continue with the program that is working for me. Will you help me, by asking me about my progress and giving me encouragement?"

To Brandy's surprise her mom said, "Yes, I can do that. I'm happy that you have lost six pounds, and I hope that over time you can get to the weight you'd like to be. I know you would feel better about yourself if you lose the amount of weight you want to lose."

Brandy said, "Thank you for saying that. I will feel great if I can lose weight and keep it off."

Brandy and her mom agreed to do a little shopping. At the end of the visit with her mom, Brandy felt neither hurt nor angry. She had learned that her thoughts, and not her mother's words and actions truly determined how she felt. For the first time she could remember, Brandy felt empowered rather than victimized following her visit with her mom.

I really hope you will practice mindfulness in a number of different ways. Please practice using the STOP skill and responding mindfully when you experience conflict with someone else. Mindful responding can empower you and bring peace of mind into your life.

Activities to Build Psychological Strength

1. Understand the value of having good habits and doing things automatically. It is helpful to brush your teeth and do many things automatically without having to use a lot of mental effort to accomplish the task.

2. Understand the value of being mindful. We live life more fully when we are focused on what is going on right now. Mindfulness involves being aware of what we are experiencing in the present moment without judging.

3. Learn to observe your emotions as they occur. The first step to better managing our emotions is to be aware of them and name them when they happen. Practice recognizing and accurately naming your feelings.

4. Use the describe skill to factually describe what you experience. Often an individual makes up stories in his or her mind that are inaccurate and trigger negative emotions. Practice describing situations in a factual manner free of judgments and assumptions.

5. Practice using non-judgmental stance to calm your emotions. Persons frequently intensify their negative emotions when they make judgments that are not based on facts.

6. Use the STOP skill when your negative emotions are triggered and you experience harmful urges. Remember to stop before making things worse, to take slow and deep breaths, to realistically explore options, and to proceed with caution and respect.

7. Practice mindfulness on a daily basis. There are many health benefits of meditation. Practice mindfulness for ten to twenty minutes every day. Also practice doing daily activities non-judgmentally and one mindfully.

Chapter 9: Self-Worth and Confidence

Performing Routine Maintenance

SECRET: Developing daily habits of practicing gratitude, setting and achieving goals, reading personal affirmations, and building positive relationships are needed to sustain confidence and healthy self-worth.

I have written this chapter to help you build your confidence and self-worth so you will experience happiness and be able to perform at a higher level. Many have experienced verbal abuse, frequent criticism, and traumatic events that have severely crippled their self-esteem and belief in themselves. This chapter will focus on teaching you ways to develop healthy self-esteem, and then show you what to do to maintain it. If you fail to do simple steps to maintain your self-worth, it will decline.

Performing Routine Maintenance

There was a car commercial that had the catch phrase, "You can pay me now or pay me later." If you don't change the oil in your car and do other routine maintenance, problems will surely develop and your car will not perform optimally. It is much wiser to pay for routine oil changes, than have to pay to overhaul or replace an engine. We also need to do routine activities to maintain our psychological health.

In chapter one, you learned about the benefits of taking care of your body. Regular exercise, eating healthy foods, and having good sleep hygiene will lead to improved physical health and psychological strength. In chapter two, you were introduced to the concept of the ***protective child mindset.*** You learned that this mindset is at the root of many of our psychological problems, and were informed that simple awareness of it can contribute to psychological strength and healthy self-esteem. You also read about the benefits of accepting full responsibility for your thoughts, feelings and behavior. The advantages of having a healthy morning routine were discussed in chapter five.

In this chapter, you will discover that there are two activities that you can use to enhance your self-esteem. The benefit of setting meaningful goals will be discussed. You will be given a simple tool to change negative beliefs that lower your self-esteem. The benefits of practicing gratitude and developing personal affirmations will be explored. Before concluding the chapter, you will be helped to understand the importance of building healthy relationships to enhance your self-worth and happiness.

Major Obstacles to Healthy Self-Esteem

The following are major obstacles to healthy self-esteem and confidence:

1. ***Faulty negative beliefs*** that often start in childhood can hinder self-esteem. Examples are: "I'm not very bright," "I'm a bad person," and "No one likes me."

2. ***Blaming others*** prevents us from taking responsibility for our actions and contributes to a sense of victimhood. It is extremely difficult to feel good about ourselves when we are blaming others.

3. ***Habits of procrastination and avoidance*** are a major obstacle to healthy self-worth. It is almost impossible to feel good about ourselves when we habitually put off things that are of importance.

4. ***Lack of motivation and passion*** lessens a sense of confidence and self-esteem. Failure to set daily goals, depression, inactivity, poor physical self-care, and not making time to have fun can all add to decreased motivation.

5. ***Inadequate emotional support*** from others is yet another obstacle to self-worth and belief in oneself. Persons who have a partner, close friends, and family

support are better equipped to handle the struggles of life and enjoy healthy self-esteem.

Two Ways to Build Self-Worth

I only know of two ways to build your self-esteem or self-worth. The first way is to do things that are consistent with what you value and with the image of the person you want to be. The second way is to change negative patterns of thinking and negative beliefs, and replace them with more positive and rational beliefs. Self-esteem is built by changing your actions and thoughts.

Once you understand that you need to change both your thoughts and behavior to have healthy self-worth, you are on the road to positive change. Decide whether you need to start working first on changing your thoughts or changing your behavior. If your self-critical thinking is so intense that you never seem to feel good about yourself, then you probably need to start on changing your thinking. On the other hand, if you are self-accepting but seldom act in a way that builds your character or benefits others, then it would make sense to start work on changing your behavior.

Develop Realistic Expectations

Do you have unrealistic expectations for yourself? I'm not asking if you have worthy goals that you may never achieve. I am asking do you try to accomplish too much in any given day? When you fail to meet those expectations do you mentally batter yourself? It will be difficult, if not impossible, to develop high self-esteem as long as you expect way more of yourself than you can possibly do.

Remember to work on developing your personal courage to be imperfect. Then work on distinguishing healthy and challenging goals from unrealistic and unnecessary goals. Challenging goals require us to push a little harder, and when we attain them we feel a sense of accomplishment. Unrealistic goals are often unattainable without sacrificing other goals of equal or greater importance. Find that middle path between setting an excessive number of goals and going through life void of goals and purpose.

Selecting Important Goals

Almost every day of our life we have goals that are spoken or unspoken and goals written or not written. Many people find it helpful to share their goals with others or to write them out, and they are more likely to meet those goals if they do. Others may do well without having to commit goals to paper or screen.

In chapter five, you learned how to set effective goals. However, you were not told how to prioritize your goals. There are goals that need to be met to prevent negative consequences, and then there are goals that need to be met because they will provide positive consequences to others and yourself. If we only focus on doing chores and work, then we will miss out on more important life goals.

Six Areas of Daily Goal Setting

As a therapist I often encourage depressed clients to set daily goals. I explain that inactivity, procrastination, and isolation fuel depression. I often give depressed clients a handout titled, Setting Daily Goals. It is my belief that setting daily goals can decrease depression and enhance feelings of happiness and wellbeing.

The following are the six goal areas that are briefly explained in the daily goal setting handout:

1. **Physical Health** refers to goals that strengthen our body or improve our physical health. Going for a walk, biking, eating healthy foods, improving sleep hygiene, or going to the dentist are examples of physical health goals.

2. **Mental Health** involves setting goals that push us to learn new ideas. Taking a community education class, reading a book, researching a topic on the internet, or attending a seminar could all be examples of mental health goals.

3. **Spiritual Health** relates to goals that strengthen our relationship with God or contribute to a sense of being more alive and connected to others in a loving or compassionate manner. Doing volunteer work, enjoying nature, showing love to our children, reading an inspiring or spiritual book, prayer, and mediation

are each examples of potential goals to improve our spiritual health.

4. **Positive Interaction** involves making time to be with others. When we encourage others, or do simple acts of kindness we tend to build our own self-esteem.

5. **Recreation** is intentionally doing things that are fun or enjoyable alone or with others. If we fail to make time to have fun, we will be missing out on something important in life. Having fun is a good antidote to resentment.

6. **Completing Responsibilities** relates to doing routine tasks that need done. It is quite difficult to have healthy self-esteem when we fail to do important chores that we know need completed.

Simple Method of Changing Faulty Beliefs

In chapter three, you learned about **3 Rational Questions** and **Automatic Negative Thoughts (ANTS)** and related strategies that can be used to change your negative beliefs. When you have a pattern of thinking that is ineffective or faulty, try the following two-step technique to combat that negative belief.

1. Label the thought as a "silly thought" or "untrue belief" as soon as it enters your mind.

2. Replace the negative thought with a more rational or effective way of thinking.

Here are a couple examples of how to use this simple skill to correct negative beliefs. In the first scenario, Dave has the belief, **"No *one wants to hang around me*.**" After some reflection, he recognizes that this belief contributes to his social anxiety and to having difficulty speaking to people he doesn't know. He decides a more reasonable belief would be, "***If I allow people to get to know me, they might like me and possibly become my friend.***" Later that day Dave sees a couple guys in the cafeteria he'd like to meet, but he becomes anxious as the belief that no one would want to hang out with him creeps into his mind. He immediately thinks to himself, "That's an untrue belief." He then goes over and introduces himself, and asks if he can join the two guys for lunch. Soon they were conversing, and Dave was proud of himself for not letting his irrational belief prevent him from reaching out to someone he didn't know.

In the second scenario, Mary tends to be a huge worrier. Although she always locks the door before leaving her apartment, she will check it repeatedly. There have been times she has driven home, because she has the nagging thought in her mind that she left the front door unlocked. After reading about the technique of labeling her irrational thought and replacing it with a rational thought, she was able to do the following. As she approached the grocery store ten minutes from her home she had the following thought, ***"I think I may have forgotten to lock the front door."*** She immediately said to herself, ***"That's just another one of my silly worry thoughts. I always lock the front door, and if I***

didn't; it is highly unlikely someone would find my door unlocked the short time I'll be at the store." Her anxiety eased and Mary was able to finish her shopping.

It is easy to see how Dave's belief directly affected his self-esteem, but it is more difficult to see how Mary's worry thought about the door not being locked affected her self-worth. Like so many negative beliefs, Mary's thought (I think I may have forgotten to lock the front door) does not directly lower her self-esteem. But it triggers similar thoughts that do. Here are some of the related thoughts she may have had. ***"I worry about everything." "I am an idiot for checking this door over and over." "Anyone who would see me do this; would know I'm crazy."*** These related thoughts would certainly hurt her self-esteem.

This technique will not work for everyone, but it may work for you if you practice it on some of your less tightly held negative beliefs first. As you try it repeatedly on easier beliefs to refute, you may find that it can chip away at the more tightly held beliefs that rob you of your confidence and attack your self-worth.

Ways to Maintain Healthy Self-Esteem

I would like to strongly encourage you to use the following four strategies to maintain your confidence and self-worth.

Practicing gratitude can reduce your stress and over time help you build and maintain healthy self-esteem. Writing personal affirmations and reviewing them daily is beneficial. Continuing to engage in positive actions consistent with your personal affirmations will help you maintain your self-worth. Finally, developing positive relationships and encouraging others will enhance your confidence and self-esteem.

Gratitude Practice

Practicing gratitude is the first step I would encourage you to take to maintain your self-esteem. Take time to be grateful for your health. As you go for a walk thank your heart for pumping your life sustaining blood. Thank your eyes for allowing you to see the beautiful sky, trees, and birds. Thank your ears for the sound of birds singing, and for hearing the approaching car before you cross the street. Thank your legs and feet that take you so many different places.

Be grateful for your mind that allows you to reason and make good choices. Appreciate your loving heart that allows you to care and connect with others. Recognize your talents and strengths that enable you to go through life without being completely overwhelmed. Practicing gratitude allows you to focus more on your blessings than your weaknesses and problems.

Personal Affirmations Help Maintain Self-Esteem

Writing and reading personal and meaningful affirmations is a second step to maintaining confidence and good self-esteem. I would suggest writing five to ten affirmations and reading them every morning, and every night before you go to bed. Reading them in the morning will help you to focus on the person you wish to be that day. Reading them a second time before going to bed can allow you to reflect on any steps you have taken that day to fulfill your desire to be the type of person you want to be.

Do not write totally unrealistic affirmations you cannot believe about yourself. I would not write, "I am the healthiest person in the world." I would write, "I eat healthy foods, and enjoy consuming more vegetables and fruits. I feel good about my gradual weight loss and improved lab results." The second affirmation is true, and my weight loss and lower cholesterol levels validate my affirmation.

I would encourage you to write affirmations that touch on physical health, emotional health, happiness, positive relationships, spiritual growth and productivity. I will write a few examples for each of the above categories.

Physical Health

I exercise daily and enjoy walking, working out, and playing tennis.

I eat lots of fruits and vegetables and I eat only at meal times.

I do daily meditation to relax my body, quiet my mind, and to improve my brain and body health.

Emotional Health

I exercise regularly and get at least seven hours of sleep each night to help me maintain a positive emotional state.

I recognize and correct negative beliefs that tend to create excessive worry or self-loathing.

I focus on doing activities that help me to feel good about myself and life.

Happiness

I am happy and grateful for this day and my life, and I will allow myself to find happiness in simple things.

I enjoy bringing happiness to others by being kind in both my words and actions.

As I focus my awareness on the present moment, I experience less worry and more joy.

Positive Relationships

I strive to be honest, direct, and respectful in my interactions with everyone I meet.

I am a good listener and take time to show others I understand their thoughts and feelings.

I can learn something from every person I meet.

Spirituality

I am grateful for a loving and caring God.

I take time each day to thank God for his blessings, and to ask for guidance to accept things I cannot control.

I open my mind and heart to my loving God and allow him to work through me.

Productivity

I take time today to prioritize what is more important for me to do. I realize that there are going to be tasks that may not be fun, but need to be done.

I do more of what is important, and spend less time doing things that bring little reward to me or others.

I feel good when I set meaningful goals and focus on accomplishing them.

Positive Actions Maintain Self-Esteem

Setting daily goals that are consistent with what we value and the character we want to develop is essential to maintaining our self-esteem. If we affirm that we are a honest and fair person, and we cheat someone out of money then our actions are inconsistent with our values. Our dishonest behavior will lessen our self-esteem. If on the other hand the waitress gives us $10 too much in change, and we immediately correct the mistake in a kind way - then our self-esteem will rise.

Decide what type of person you ideally want to be, and then act in a way that is consistent with your ideal. When you stumble, take responsibility for your failure and do what you can to correct the mistake or wrongful action. Be a person of integrity.

Here are some general guidelines for acting in a way that will maintain your self-worth. Strive to encourage others, and to point out positive qualities and actions in others. Be kind in what you say and do. Be generous and also accept graciously the kindness and helpfulness that others. Do simple acts of kindness. Be honest so others will be able to trust you. Be respectful and make it a habit to pause before you speak so your words will be mindful.

Positive Relationships and Self-Worth

The persons you choose to spend time with will be most important in helping you to maintain your self-esteem. Strive to spend more time with persons who are positive and hopeful. Spend less time with persons who speak and act in ways that are overly critical.

I would like to share a poem I wrote that I often give clients who are spending too much time with people who are negative and overly critical.

Bobbers and Sinkers

In life there are two types of people-
bobbers and sinkers.
Bobbers are persons who listen and encourage,
while sinkers are just stinkers.
Sinkers always look for the worst in others
and skillfully bring it out.
They judge, blame, manipulate with guilt,
and scream and shout.
Sinkers themselves feel so low they never wish
to see another rise,
So their negative outlook and harsh criticism
are of little surprise.
Bobbers are the people I truly want to
hang around,
Because acceptance and good humor
in them abound.
No matter how discouraged and frustrated
you may feel,
Bobbers lift you up with encouragement
that is genuine and real.
Unless you want to sink to the bottom and
settle into mire,
I suggest you seek out bobbers - affirming
persons you admire.

Spending time with persons who share your positive values and validate you will do much to help you maintain your self-worth. You do not have to divorce family members and friends who tend to be negative, but you could benefit from learning to not take what they say personally. You may also profit from making more time for positive people you know that lift you up, as you make less time for those who tend to pull you down into the mire of negativity.

Activities to Build Psychological Strength

1. Build your self-esteem through positive actions and changing your self-critical thinking. Visualize the type of person you want to be, and start acting that way. Label your self-critical beliefs as untrue and replace them with healthy beliefs.

2. Develop realistic expectations. Accept that you have a limited amount of willpower at any given time, and don't set goals so high that you will never meet them. Realize that it is better to finish one project than to start ten great projects you never complete.

3. Set meaningful goals. Set goals that are consistent with what you value and that will lead to a sense of accomplishment. You may need to do things like tidying up and fixing a healthy meal before working on a higher goal of writing on a book.

4. Practice gratitude. Be grateful for your talents, health, and relationships. Focusing on gratitude will enhance your self-worth.

5. Write and daily read affirmations that are personal and meaningful. Write 3 to 8 affirmations that identify the person you want to be, and then visualize being that person. Ideally read these affirmations at the start of your day and once again before bedtime to reflect on what you did that day that was consistent with your affirmations.

6. Develop habits of positive behavior. A wise use of willpower would be to gradually develop habits that will sustain us. These habits may include a daily routine of exercise, reading every day to learn new things, and acting in a way that is kind and validating of others.

7. Form positive relationships. One of the best ways to maintain positive self-esteem is to develop relationships with positive persons who will validate and emotionally support you. Learn to spend more time with persons who encourage you and less time with persons who pull you down.

Chapter 10: Discovering More Happiness

Enjoying the Drive

SECRET: Happiness comes not from the accumulation of wealth and material things, but rises out of an attitude of gratitude, eagerness to learn, acceptance of oneself and others as they are, and living life with a purpose that blesses others.

I hope by the time you have come to this chapter that you have already started feeling happier as a result of using some of the ideas and strategies that have been presented. Happiness is experienced more when we are mindful, grateful, and have worked to develop positive relationships with others. In this chapter, you will be shown a number of paths to experiencing a more fulfilling and happy life. Being psychologically strong leads to happiness.

Enjoy the Drive

My wife and I love to travel and we enjoy visiting national parks. Rocky Mountain National Park is one of our favorite places to vacation. Several years ago, we drove up Trail Ridge Road in early October when the Aspen had turned golden in color. It was the first time we had been there to witness the transformation of the deciduous trees to their fall colors blending with the dark green of the conifer.

Frequently, I pulled onto the roadside parking areas to admire the beauty of the scenery and to snap photos that would in the future help me to remember the breathtaking views. Some people drive quickly through the Park and fail to experience the awe that nature offers. I was able to photograph mountain peaks, elk, chipmunks, and the beautiful aspen intermingled with pine and fir trees.

In life we can be so caught up in completing some task or getting somewhere that we fail to enjoy the journey. This chapter is devoted to giving you some practical ideas for experiencing more joy in your life. It is a roadmap for taking the scenic route, instead of speeding down the interstate highway that the majority of people travel.

Practice Gratitude

Living life in a spirit of gratitude is one of the most important ways to experience happiness. My father survived the great depression, and he lived his life in the spirit of gratitude. I believe it helped him to be a kind and giving person, and enabled him to develop resilience. He cared for my mother after she became a victim of Alzheimer's. I did not once hear my dad complain during the years that my mother slowly lost her ability to take care of herself and to communicate.

When my mother died at the age of 85, I feared my father might soon follow her. He was able to move forward with his life and lived another ten years until he died of a heart attack at age 95. He was never bitter, and he enjoyed going trout fishing with me on numerous occasions after mom died. I believe his faith and gratitude served him well.

In the previous chapter, gratitude practice was suggested to be a tool that can help us build a sense of self-worth. It helps to ground us and avoid excessive worry. I have found it to be an antidote to both anxiety and depression.

Persons often feel good when they take the time to thoughtfully make a gratitude list of various people, blessings, and experiences that have enriched their life. Research studies in positive psychology have shown that writing three new things people are grateful for every day for a month increases their feelings of happiness. It helps people to focus more on the positive and less on the negative.

Silver Lining Thinking

Gratitude has more to do with how we look at life than what happens to us. It is a good practice to be honest about our feelings, and then to express gratitude for something of value that can come out almost any situation. I call this "Silver Lining Thinking." It helps us to take a middle path and avoid becoming stuck in a cycle of negative thinking and misery.

I have found that Silver Lining Thinking helps me to be happier, because it allows me to see another side of a difficult situation. When good things happen it also helps me to savor positive events. I have developed a simple worksheet that I have shared with a number of clients. A person using the worksheet would simply fill in the two lines below to describe how they honestly feel about a given situation, and write something they are grateful for in that situation.

I honestly feel ____________________________

____

and I'm grateful for _____________________________

____.

The following are examples to help you understand what Silver Lining Thinking entails. I challenge you to think about what you might honestly feel, and what you might be grateful for in each situation.

Jim is beginning to feel quite anxious before giving an important speech. He takes a few calming breaths and thinks the following. ***I honestly feel very anxious, and I'm grateful that I'm prepared to give my speech and that my family will love and support me regardless of how well my speech goes.***

Jennifer is giving her three-year-old daughter a birthday party, and her daughter is having a good time. Jennifer thinks, ***I'm feel great and I'm having an awesome time, and I'm grateful that Emily is so happy and is getting along with her little friends.***

Jason is pulled over for going 78 in a 70-mph zone on the interstate. After the police officer writes out a ticket, he thinks: ***I'm frustrated for getting this ticket and for having to deal with it when I return from our vacation, and I'm grateful that I role modeled responsible behavior for my kids by being respectful to the officer.***

Beverly is told by her sister that Uncle William died from a heart attack. She thinks: ***I'm sad that Uncle Bill died and I feel for his wife and three children, and I'm happy for his influence in my life and how he touched the lives of so many people with his kindness and helpfulness.***

Jen finds out that her car is going to need a new transmission. She thinks: ***I'm angry that I will need to pay out a large amount of money on car repairs I hadn't anticipated, and I'm grateful that I have good credit and that Jane will take me to and from work while my car is in the shop.***

Wilson receives a glowing performance appraisal at the end of his probationary period at his new job. He thinks: ***I feel relieved and proud about what my boss said, and I'm thankful that I have worked hard and have offered creative solutions that my boss feels can be implemented.***

I encourage you to try Silver Lining Thinking out. *It has been my experience that using silver lining thinking prevents us from ruminating and spiraling into a pattern of negative thinking. I would challenge you to use it. In unpleasant situations, be sure to honestly identify your emotions before looking for something good you have to be grateful for in that situation. In pleasant situations, allow yourself to savor your positive feelings by recognizing what you are most grateful for in that event.*

Be More Active

I have found that I can easily sink into a state of complacency. My happiness level tends to sink low when I become inactive and spend too much time sitting and watching TV. I strive to get some exercise every day, even if it just going for a short walk. Being outdoors and appreciating the beauty of nature gives me joy.

I have found playing racquetball is a good cardio exercise that I enjoy. As was discussed in chapter one, adults benefit from having at least 150 minutes of exercise a week. Exercise reduces depression and stress, and improves the quality of our life. People who exercise regularly live longer, and I believe are happier.

Get off the couch and do something you enjoy. See a movie, go to the zoo, visit a museum, or go for a scenic drive. Realize the benefits of exercise by swimming, biking, kayaking, hiking, playing tennis, or join a team sport. You may discover that the only thing you have to lose by being more active is a few pounds.

Tidy Up Your Environment

You might be surprised that the simple act of tidying up an area in the house where you spend a lot of time can make you feel better. I challenge you to tidy up your office, kitchen, or living room. It may not be fun to do it, but notice how you feel when it is completed. Most people feel noticeably better when they have brightened up an area of their living environment.

Take it another step by adding something to the living space that lifts your spirits. You may want to add a framed photo of a favorite vacation spot, or a framed picture of a loved one. You may want to purchase a plant, put out a vase of cut flowers, or purchase a piece of art. Make your home a place that brings you a sense of peace and happiness. If possible do the same for your work space.

Be Quick to Show Kindness

Greeting someone with a smile and cheerful words not only puts a smile on their face, but it also brings you joy. Persons who show kindness and caring to others are richer for doing so. Some mistakenly believe that they can enhance their self-esteem by judging others as being less than themselves. In doing this they generate negative feelings, and ultimately feel worse.

One way of being kind is to show encouragement to others. Encouragement involves acknowledging the strengths and positive actions of another. It may be something as simple as saying, "Wow, your weight loss program must be working well for you. You look great." And it might be deeper and sound something like this. "I know it has been a real struggle for you losing your mother. I'm amazed as to how you have kept going for your children, and know there have been times where you reached deep inside to drag yourself out of bed. I admire you for how hard you've worked, and I want you to know if you need me to watch the kids or do something for you, I would be more than happy to help."

Simple acts of kindness can be opening a door for someone, being gracious while driving, or letting someone with a few grocery items go ahead of you. Practice being kind just for the sake of doing so.

Avoid telling others about it, unless you are using it as a teaching example for your children. Notice how you feel when you take time out from your busy day to just be nice.

Plan Something You Look Forward to Doing

There are times that anticipating doing something fun may generate more joy and excitement than actually doing it. It is rare when I don't have some activity planned that I'm looking forward to doing. I may be thinking about the next time I'll go fishing, anticipating the family vacation to Yellowstone National Park, or simply thinking about the walk I'll take later today.

I would encourage you to plan fun activities you will do alone, and other things you will do with family and friends. It is okay to do a little daydreaming from time to time. It is often fun to talk with others about some event you look forward to doing together. What are some positive activities you are looking forward to experiencing?

Spend Time with Positive People

In the previous chapter, you were made aware of the importance of surrounding yourself with positive people to help you build and maintain a healthy self-esteem. Having positive relationships is also a key for being happy. Who do you have in your life that is a "bobber"? It is important to find supportive people who encourage and validate you.

We can build positive relationships by treating others the way we wish to be treated. Work at being an active listener who is in touch with how other people feel. Show interest in the areas in their life that are most important to them. It may be their children, career, a sporting event, or what they do for recreation. Ask questions about what matters most to them. Strive to be open and share about what is important to you. Be supportive not only in your words, but also in your actions.

It is important to spend less time with persons who tend to be negative and judgmental. You may have family members that are that way. Work on accepting them as they are, and accept that they are probably doing the best they can with their experience and the beliefs they hold. You don't have to avoid them completely, but you do need to learn how to be around them without allowing their negativity to pull you down or enrage you.

Intentionally look for persons that are positive in both their words and actions. Having just a few positive relationships in your life can enhance your happiness. Make a genuine effort to develop relationships with persons who are going to lift your spirit, and help motivate you to achieve meaningful goals.

Follow Work with Play

I believe it is each individual's responsibility to make time to have fun. Attempt to find a balance between work and play. Excessive work without play often leads to burnout and feelings of resentment. Excessive play with little work may lead others to feel resentment toward you, and makes it difficult for you to feel good when you do little to contribute.

I have found in my life, that I feel happier when I follow work with some form of play. If I work hard by mowing the lawn and tending the garden, I will often play by walking to the neighborhood lake and fishing. After I have spent 30 minutes to an hour writing, I will often play a couple video games on my computer for fun. After I complete my morning routine of reading, silence, affirmations, and journaling, I will follow it with mindfully eating a tasty breakfast.

Eagerness to Learn

Having a curious mind and openness to learning contribute to one's happiness. I enjoy seeing persons at any age who delight in discovery. It is fun seeing my five-year-old granddaughter and two-year-old grandson showing excitement in seeing a new animal at the zoo or aquarium. I believe that some people are lucky enough to relish learning new things even in their eighties and nineties.

I would encourage you to keep an active mind and read books, peruse articles of interest on the internet, visit museums, and travel. Talk to persons and show interest in hearing their stories. When traveling, make it a point to visit sites of interest off the beaten path. While going for a walk, be mindful of what you experience. Today while I walked I was mindful of hearing a crow, a "barking" squirrel, the chirping of crickets, and other sounds of nature.

Study areas that you're most interested in learning. I am often drawn to learning about mindfulness, positive psychology, space travel, and spiritual practices. Spend time reading about topics that are exiting to you. Be grateful for the availability of so much knowledge at our fingertips.

Acceptance Leads to Happiness

I often tell my clients the most stressful word in the English language is ***should***. We are quick to become frustrated and judgmental toward others when they fail to do what we think they ***should do***. We also are quick to be self-critical when we fail to do what we think we ***should do***, or we do something we believe we ***shouldn't do.***

It is quite difficult to feel happy when we are thinking critical thoughts of oneself or others. "Should thinking" often robs us of peace of mind and happiness. Accepting reality as it is makes it possible for us to be less frustrated and to have more peace of mind. When we let go of trying to change others, then we also have more peace of mind and less conflict.

We have the right to ask other people to treat us with respect or to stop acting in a self-destructive way. If we have a friend or family member with a drinking problem that lashes out at us in anger when drunk, we certainly have the right to make them aware of how their abusive words are hurtful to us and request that they stop. ***But if we get caught up in thinking they <u>should stop drinking if they love us</u>, then it is easy to get stuck in a battle of trying to change them when they're not wanting to change.*** Accepting that they have a drinking problem and are unlikely to change is a crucial step for us to do something different that will safeguard us should they continue drinking and being verbally abusive.

It is also important to realize that we are not supposed to be happy all the time. Life is at times a struggle, and facing challenges helps us to mature and to develop character. We can have little pride in doing something that is simple and does not involve hard work. Raising children is not an easy task, and thus we find happiness by winning battles of endurance. Parents of infants learn to function in spite of sleep deprivation. They learn they can change a messy diaper, even if they are sick. Later they learn they can control their temper, even if their young child throws a horrific temper tantrum.

There would be little challenge to running a marathon, if one could simply dress in running attire and complete a 26.2 mile run with no discomfort or battle of mind over body. It is that battle of mind over body, that brings deep satisfaction to those who train and complete a marathon. Frequently, successful struggle in one area builds confidence, and can easily run over into other areas. It is not hiding from challenges that brings us happiness. It is facing challenges head on and overcoming them that leads to happiness.

Living with Purpose

I believe living life with purpose is essential to experiencing and maintaining a higher level of happiness. Your purpose will evolve as you go through life, but merely seeking wealth or pleasure becomes empty. We may experience fun without living with purpose, but we will not feel that sense of accomplishment and depth of feeling that comes when we live life with passion and meaningful goals.

Living life with purpose may involve seeking knowledge, or doing well in a career that benefits others. It may involve being a good parent, or being a teacher that enjoys seeing children learn. It might be overcoming one's substance abuse, and sharing one's story to help others overcome their addiction. It could be knowing God through spiritual practice, and showing compassion and caring to others in a specific way. It could be protecting others as a law enforcement officer, or it could be doing mission work. You will be happier if you find a purpose that is meaningful to you.

I would like to share a poem I've written on happiness. My hope is that it will bring a smile to your face.

Happiness

If I tried to define happiness, I'm sure
I would lose some of it.
It cannot be caught and held captive in a jar,
like a firefly brightly lit.
Happiness is always a welcome friend that
makes life brighter,
And it seems to come when I'm less serious -
when things are seen lighter.
I cannot wait on the couch and simply hope
it will appear,
For it's not something I'm entitled to
and this is clear.
I cannot win it in a lottery or buy it
with a lot of money,
And I'm more likely to find it by doing
something funny.
Sometimes it comes to me when I've
completed work,
And at other times it may visit me when I
meet a friendly clerk.
If in my selfishness I try to hide it away
and keep it all to myself,
It quickly disappears as does a leprechaun
or frightened little elf.
When I share it with family and friends
and freely give it away,
Happiness grows stronger and I find
more time to play.
I have learned to appreciate happiness
for what it is.
Like Alka-Seltzer in a glass of water -
it gives life its fizz.

I hope that reading this book has helped you identify a purpose for living that not only contributes to your personal growth, but also benefits others in some way. I would encourage you to take a moment to reflect on ways that you have become a psychologically stronger person. What have you learned that has helped you to be a happier and healthier individual? What are areas where you need to focus your attention to increase your strength? How have the changes you've made benefited others?

This is not the end, but rather it is a beginning for you to make changes that can transform your life and help you experience greater happiness and peace of mind. If this book has been helpful to you, please share it with others so they too can learn secrets of psychological strength.

Activities to Build Psychological Strength

1. Practice gratitude by making a gratitude list. Take some time to write out a list of various things you are most grateful to have. The list could include people you value, your health, personal strengths, important possessions, pets, your faith or spirituality, freedoms, and beautiful places you've been.

2. Use silver lining thinking to stop negativity in its tracks. When you experience negative emotions, honestly write how you feel and what you are grateful for in that situation.

3. Be more active. Enhance your happiness by doing more activities. When possible reap the benefits of physical exercise by hiking, canoeing, playing competitive sports, or engaging in other exercise.

4. Tidy up the places where you spend more time. The simple task of getting your desk in order, picking up the family room, or cleaning the kitchen can help you experience more peace of mind and happiness.

5. Show kindness to others. Strive to be kind and helpful to others and you will make friends and experience more happiness.

6. Spend time with positive people. Choosing to interact with positive people can lift your spirits and motivate you to grow.

7. Live life with a purpose. Identify several areas of life where you want to grow and hope to help others. Visualize living your life with passion and purpose.

References

Achor, Shawn, *Before Happiness,* (New York, Crown Business, 2013)

Achor, Shawn, *The Happiness Advantage,* (New York, Crown Business, 2010)

Altman, Donald, *Living Kindness,* (Oregon City, Moon Lake Media, 2003)

Altman, Donald, *One Minute Mindfulness,* (Novato, California, New World Library, 2011)

Amen, Daniel G., M.D., *The Amen Solution,* (New York, Three Rivers Press, 2011)

Amen, Daniel G., M.D., *Use Your Brain to Change Your Age,* (New York, Harmony, 2012)

Baumeister, Roy F. & Tierney, John, *Willpower,* (London, Penguin Books, 2012)

Bowen, Will, *Happy This Year,* (Grand Haven, MI, Grand Harbor Press, 2013)

Elrod, Hal, *The Miracle Morning,* (Hal Elrod International, Inc. 2012)

Fralich, Terry, *Cultivating Lasting Happiness: A 7-Step Guide to Mindfulness,* (Eau Claire, WI, Pesi, 2007)

Fredrickson, Barbara L., Ph.D., *Positivity,* (New York, Three Rivers Press, 2009)

Hanh, Thich Nhat, *Happiness: Essential Mindfulness Practices,* (Berkely, CA, Parallex Press, 2009)

Hanson, Rick, Ph.D., *Hardwiring Happiness,* (New York, Harmony, 2013)

Hawn, Goldie, *10 Minute Mindfulness,* (New York, Penguin Group, 2011)

Ilardi, Stephen S., Ph.D., *The Depression Cure,* (Cambridge, MA, Da Capo Press, 2009)

Johnson, Lynn D., Ph.D., *Enjoy Life: Healing with Happiness,* (Salt Lake City, Head Acre Press, 2008)

Johnson, Lynn D., Ph.D., *The Healing Power of Sleep,* (Salt Lake City, Head Acre Press, 2009)

Kegan, Robert & Lahey, Lisa Laskow, *Immunity to Change,* (Boston, Harvard Business Press, 2009)

Linehan, Marsha M., Ph.D., *Cognitive Behavioral Treatment of Borderline Personality Disorder*, (New York, Guilford Press, 1993)

Linehan, Marsha M., *DBT Skills Training Manual, 2nd. Edition,* (New York, Guilford Press, 2015)

Oplin, Dr. Michael & Bracken, Sam, *Unwind: 7 Principles for a Stress-Free Life,* (Grand Harbor Press, 2014)

Pucci, Dr. Aldo R., *Feel the Way You Want to Feel... No Matter What,* (New York, iUniverse, Inc. 2010)

Pucci, Dr. Aldo R., *The Client's Guide to Cognitive-Behavioral Therapy,* (New York, iUniverse, Inc. 2006)

Seligman, Martin E. P., *Authentic Happiness,* (New York, Free Press, 2002)

Seligman, Martin E. P., *Flourish,* (New York, Free Press, 2011)

Stone, Douglas, Patton, Bruce, and Heen, Sheila, *Difficult Conversations,* (New York, Penguin Books, 2010)

Taitz, Jennifer L., *End Emotional Eating,* (Oakland, New Harbinger Publications, 2012)

Thompson, Susan Peirce, Ph.D., *Bright Line Eating*, (Carlsbad, CA, Hay House, 2017)